Starting With Zero

Rev. Kathryn L. Smith

Author of
There Is Fire In The Blood, Meet Me On The Mountain, Wilt Thou Be Made Whole, I Hear the Rocks Falling and I Am Who God Says I Am

PUBLISHED by PARABLES
Earthly Stories with a Heavenly Meaning

Starting With Zero
Rev. Kathryn L. Smith

Published By Parables
November, 2018

All Rights Reserved. No part of this book may be reproduced or utilized in any form or by any means, electronic or mechanical, including photocopying, recording, or by any information storage and retrieval system, without permission in writing from the author.

    ISBN 978-1-945698-75-0
    Printed in the United States of America

Readers should be aware that Internet Web sites offered as citations and/or sources for further information may have been changed or disappeared between the time this was written and the time it is read.

Table of Contents

5	It's All About Fear
17	Something from Nothing
31	The Blood has your Name on it
43	Holy Oil in Clay Vessels
55	Not Nearly Enough
65	Ground Zero
75	Look Through the Nail Print
89	What is in Your Hand?
97	Making Bread and Wine
107	Fishing with Jesus
113	Starting at Dead
127	Lazarus Come Forth
149	Supernatural Supply
163	Surrounded
179	Lost Puzzle Pieces
186	Works Cited
188	Author Page

Acknowledgements

It is with great respect and admiration that I dedicate this book to Rev. Lisa Naylor. She is a woman of faith who has shown that the blood can fully change any person. Her salvation and her love for Scripture are evident in everything she does. She is passionate about souls and walks in deep love; through sorrow and joy she has proven that the Lord is her fortress. I pray that my life is as influential and meaningful as hers.

I deeply appreciate all those who made me the woman of faith, the minister, and the author that I am. I want to especially thank Pastor Timothy A. Naylor & Pastor Rick Naylor, who taught me what it meant to be called and how to minister. They taught me faith, and to trust in the indisputable Word of God. My pastors and other men of faith have invested in my spiritual growth and served as shepherds to my soul. I also want to express my gratitude to all the men and women whose ministries and books have shaped my faith; some of those names have faded over time, but their truths have become ingrained within my spirit; to all those who taught me and nurtured me, but were not specifically cited in this book—thank you.

I want to thank the people who so kindly and consistently encouraged me, and those who have purchased and read my books. I wish to extend special gratitude to Donna Naylor who was the first to read each of my books and who graciously did some editing. She helped me with grammar and punctuation, while always honoring the message within the text.

Thank you to my dear husband, Buzz who patiently endured countless hours alone while I ministered or wrote. He has supported and honored my calling and prayed for me. I deeply love and appreciate the man of God that he is and the constant love that he shows me.

Mostly, I want to thank the Lord Jesus Christ who loved me when I was unlovely, saved me when I was lost, called me when I was nothing and anointed me to do His work. I pray that He will be glorified and lifted high in all I have attempted for Him.

Starting With Zero

Isaiah 41: 13 (KJV) *[13] For I the LORD thy God will hold thy right hand, saying unto thee, Fear not; I will help thee.*

It's All About Fear

One of the first things that God wants us to hear is, "Do not be afraid." The actual words "Fear Not" occur in the King James Bible sixty-three times. The idea is expressed in other words about three hundred additional times. That amounts to approximately one "fear not" for every day of the year. God does not want us living in fear, but fear still plagues the masses. **Joshua 1:9 (KJV)** [9] *Have not I commanded thee? Be strong and of a good courage; be not afraid, neither be thou dismayed: for the LORD thy God is with thee whithersoever thou goest.* The enemy uses fear to drive us and control us. Fear is, in essence, the belief that something bad is about to happen. To fear is to expect loss and to anticipate disaster. Worry, anxiety, dread and apprehension are all forms of fear.

There is a reason why the devil wants us walking in fear. Fear is the polar opposite of faith. They are mutually exclusive. If we are in fear, we are not using our faith; we are vulnerable. Put your confidence in of the power of God. **Hebrews 11:6 (KJV)** *⁶ But without faith it is impossible to please him: for he that cometh to God must believe that he is, and that he is a rewarder of them that diligently seek him.* It is the devil's delight to have us worried and fearful. The strategy of our enemy is really all about fear. He desires to have us running around looking over our shoulder.

So what does that have to do with "Zero?" The devil would have us believe that we are basically worthless and powerless—nothing more than zeros. "We were taught to despise our poor efforts to perform in a way that would make us worthy of love." (Smith p. 69) We can never earn what was freely given from eternity past. For some reason, people think they have to do right, think right, and perform well, or follow rules to earn a standing with God. That could not be farther from the truth. **I John 4:16 (KJV)** *¹⁶ And we have known and believed the love that God hath to us. God is love; and he that dwelleth in love dwelleth in God, and God in him.* God's love for us is unconditional. He who is love just accepts us. Whatever obedience or effort needful for our acceptance, was accomplished in Christ and we can never add to what He has done. "You are the focus of the passionate and unconditional love of God. He loves you with His entire being. You have all of His love as if you were the only human in existence. He loves you without reference to your behavior." (Smith p. 61) **I John 4:19 (KJV)** [19] *We love him, because he first loved us.* Before we were born He loved us. While we were sinners and failures, God sought us out. **Romans 5:8 (KJV)** [8] *But God commendeth his love toward us, in that, while we were yet sinners, Christ died for us.* **Jeremiah 31:3 (KJV)** [3] *The LORD hath appeared of old unto me, saying, Yea, I have loved thee with an everlasting love: therefore with lovingkindness have I drawn thee.* Jesus thought we were worth dying for. We need to recognize that while we may be weak and frail and flawed, we are of great value to God. When we know that He truly loves us, we can stop trying to earn His love.

The devil will have us focus on what we do instead of who God is. He will tell us we are too young or too old. He will say we aren't smart enough or capable. Our enemy assaults our minds with fear of failure and fear of rejection to keep us from trying to accomplish new and difficult things. I spent the first eighteen years of my life wanting to do things that I probably could have accomplished, but I didn't try. Fear was so strong that I never tried out for a school play, joined a club or entered any contests. I did not even imagine myself going to college or holding down a job. The whole time I was in high school I was basically invisible. I always felt like I was being compared to others and coming up short. The truth is, I can preach, sing and write and I have a few other talents. I was valedictorian when I graduated from Bible College, so that lie that I wasn't smart enough got exposed. Fear held me down, but once I got saved, Jesus lifted me up. Most of us live in fear that someone will find out we are just us and we don't have all the answers; to tell you the truth, I don't even have all the questions. What I do have is a relationship with God and He is more than enough for any situation.

If the devil cannot get you troubled by the idea that you are not enough, he will tell you don't have enough. Honestly, most of us are uncomfortable with the idea of lack. Satan will try to make you stingy, clinging to what you have for fear of running out of something you dearly need. He would have you chasing after money and possessions. That spirit left unbridled will produce both workaholics and hoarders. The fear of people, like the fear of failing them, is also crippling. If allowed to go to extremes, it produces agoraphobia. If he could the devil would consume you with fear and make you unstable in all your ways. He can not. **II Timothy 1:7 (KJV)** *[7] For God hath not given us the spirit of fear; but of power, and of love, and of a sound mind.*

I am urging you fear not! In life and in ministry the enemy wants us walking around feeling insecure about our abilities and fearful that our supply will run out. He has us measuring our abilities by some arbitrary standard or in comparison with others. God made you who you are. God knows exactly what is in you and He called you anyway. He must think you are up to the task. God knows our end from the beginning and what seems like a weakness or a failure from our point of view might be part of the path it takes to get us where God wants us. **Jeremiah 29:11 (KJV)** *[11] For I know the thoughts that I think toward you, saith the LORD, thoughts of peace, and not of evil, to give you an expected end.*

Satan tries to make our problems seem big and our resources small. We have a really big God, and He is more than ready to help us through anything that comes our way. God is our Father and with His help we are totally equipped. We are enough. **Isaiah 41: 13 (KJV)** *[13] For I the LORD thy God will hold thy right hand, saying unto thee, Fear not; I will help thee.* God is not far away and inaccessible. His resources are limitless and He wants us to know that we have access to everything we need.

God intends for us to be prosperous; that is, to know we will have sufficient supply. "If you are not careful, when you think of the laws of prosperity all you will see is money—only a very small part of prosperity. True prosperity is God manifesting Himself to us in His Word" (Copeland p. 23) **Philippians 4: 19 (KJV)** [19] *But my God shall supply all your need according to his riches in glory by Christ Jesus.* That supply is not out of my bank account or my abilities; it is from the whole of His riches. He paves the streets with gold in heaven; He uses sapphires and emeralds for foundation stones in the buildings there. If I need financial support, He has it. Some of the biggest churches in America were built debt free during the great depression. That is possible only with His help.

As a teacher, my deepest desire is to know that I have heard from Him and that I present the information and revelation well. It is easy to fear that I will not make the connection for the reader. If not careful, I could misrepresent Him or leave His message unclear. That fear is anchored in the doubt that I am anointed enough and knowledgeable enough. I sometimes doubt that I will hear His voice clearly or that my opinion and impression will somehow overshadow His intent. He said I am His child and I will know His voice. **John 10: 4 (KJV)** [4] *...he goeth before them, and the sheep follow him: for they know his voice.* God will speak to us and

He will make His directions clear; we have no reason to be afraid.

Isaiah 30:20-21 (KJV) *[20] And though the Lord give you the bread of adversity, and the water of affliction, yet shall not thy teachers be removed into a corner any more, but thine eyes shall see thy teachers: [21] And thine ears shall hear a word behind thee, saying, This is the way, walk ye in it, when ye turn to the right hand, and when ye turn to the left.* When God called me to teach and to preach, I could have reacted in fear. He told me to build up the body of Christ. I realized that I don't do that out of my knowledge or my ability. All I really need to do is hear from Him and study and share what He has taught me. I do not have to be someone special, because He is and I can depend upon Him.

When I first started to teach adults, I wondered if I knew enough and I wanted to make sure that I had something that God was saying to His people. I used to write out all my Sunday school teachings in notebooks. One day when I was staring at a stack of those notebooks, I realized I really do have something to say. Shortly after that, an anointed minister prophesied over me that he could see me writing and writing. A little over a year later I published my first book. All five of the books I have published to date are teachings that I used in my own ministry. **Jeremiah 30:2 (KJV)** *[2]*

Thus speaketh the LORD God of Israel, saying, Write thee all the words that I have spoken unto thee in a book. With God's help, I became an author. I have never had to do anything on my own. Everything I have ever accomplished was a gift that He placed in me.

Philippians 4:6 (KJV) *[6] Be careful for nothing; but in everything by prayer and supplication with thanksgiving let your requests be made known unto God.* "God does not want you to be fearful, fretful or anxious…So when you have a care or worry, straightaway, turn that care or worry into prayer…In the midst of that prayer, thank God that He is already your healing, provision, good success and victory." (Prince 9/3/18)

You can accomplish anything with God's help. The most awful and crippling fear you have ever faced is the devil trying to keep you from your destiny and your full potential. If the devil is telling you that you are a zero, that's good because God can make something out of nothing every time! This teaching is my attempt to let you know that even if you feel like you are nothing and you have zero resources, God will make something amazing out of your life. He delights in starting with nothing to create something that will bring Him glory.

Our natural senses tell us that what we see and feel is real; but the truth is that our Lord and His promises are more real. The spiritual realm is much more powerful than the natural one. It is important that we recognize our source, our help, is the only One with any real power. Faith and fear strive to control our access to the spirit world, where our help is. We live in fear that we won't be healed or that it won't work for me this time. We see ourselves lacking or wanting or weak instead of loved and supplied and healed. We fear our faith is too small, that somehow this time the blood is inaccessible; fear is a total lie. His victory is already won. His revelation has already come and the power is already present. The answer is already here and the manifestation is already in the glory.

We are truly insignificant in this universe without its Creator. As true believers, we came to Christ with nothing to offer. We actually came with a sin debt that put us at a negative spiritual net worth; we started as less than zero. He takes our failure and sin and produces in us freedom and wisdom and power; we don't have to start with anything. We simply know that He is enough and then just redistribute what He has given to us. His inspiration and instructions become so clear it is like He carved them in stone. We see and feel and experience it and He pours it out of us that all can receive.

We are God's representatives on the earth, carriers of the glory—vessels of His power and presence. We are bearers of His love and anointing.

Philippians 4:13 (KJV) [13] *I can do all things through Christ which strengtheneth me.* Fear not, for with God, we are more than enough. There is no need He will not meet for us and no place for fear in us.

Starting With Zero

Hebrews 11:1-3 (KJV) *¹ Now faith is the substance of things hoped for, the evidence of things not seen. ² For by it the elders obtained a good report. ³ Through faith we understand that the worlds were framed by the word of God, so that things which are seen were not made of things which do appear.*

Something from Nothing

God is the creator of everything that exists. He made the whole of the universe out of nothing. **Hebrews 11:3 (KJV)** *³ Through faith we understand that the worlds were framed by the word of God, so that things which are seen were not made of things which do appear.* Some think the unseen things are atoms and molecules too small for us to detect but I am telling you He made those too! He made all of it from the image inside of Himself. He did not need materials to build with or some substance to start from. **Psalm 33:8-9 (NIV2011)** *⁸ Let all the earth fear the LORD; let all the people of the world revere him. ⁹ For he spoke, and it came to be; he commanded, and it stood firm.* God is totally self-sufficient.

God likes it when we just give Him a blank slate. He told Moses, "Hew me out a tablet and I will write on it!" Well, those tablets were made of stone. Stone was just hardened dirt and it was the same thing He used to make mankind. **Genesis 2:7 (KJV)** *⁷ And the LORD God formed man of the dust of the ground, and breathed into his nostrils the breath of life; and man became a living soul.* I didn't read there that God mass produced men. Did He start with 100 men? No, He created one man Adam and later gave him a mate. The Creator said, "Go and populate the earth." In 2018 the population reached 7.6 billion people. God can start with nothing and make something huge.

If you do not have any real talent or ability or knowledge, that is fine; God can work with that. Give Him your blank slate and let Him write. God is the master craftsman; He is highly skilled in making something out of nothing. **Ephesians 2:10 (KJV)** *¹⁰ For we are his workmanship, created in Christ Jesus unto good works, which God hath before ordained that we should walk in them.*

If we start with nothing, zero, what is null and void, we leave a place for Him to fill. If we are infertile and useless, He alone is the One who makes the impossible happen with us. The same God who spoke light out of darkness and life out of death looks at what appears to be nothing or seems to be impossible and sees potential. I once heard that a famous artist was asked how he knew what to make out of a piece of marble. He answered that He looked at the stone until he saw the image trapped inside it. Then he began to chip away whatever was not what he could see within himself. Eventually the shape appeared. That is what God is doing in our lives. He is chipping away at all the doubt and fear and rubbish until His masterpiece appears. He has a finished masterpiece in mind when He looks at you. It is at the place of our weakness and need that miracles occur.

I have heard it said that little is much when God is in it. That almost sounds like a seed. It might not look like much but there is great potential held inside. **Matthew 17:20 (KJV)** [20] *... If ye have faith as a grain of mustard seed, ye shall say unto this mountain, Remove hence to yonder place; and it shall remove; and nothing shall be impossible unto you.* Mustard seeds are not much bigger than the period at the end of this sentence, but they produce well. If you have even the tiniest bit of faith plant it, speak it, expect it to produce. Act as if God had guaranteed your work and your words. He produces in you and through you and for you whatever you need. Everything starts small like a seed. It is taken and buried within the earth. It seems like nothing is happening and then it springs forth greater than the seed seemed to be.

When Dean, a young man in our church, spoke recently, he told us about bamboo farmers. There are different kinds of bamboo, but one particular variety grown in China is very interesting. The farmers plant their seeds and water them and care for the soil every twelve hours for five years before they see the sprout. That is truly faith in action. No evidence, just a confidence that the seed will produce. Five years is a very long time to go without any confirmation that something is happening. Faith motivates that farmer 3650 to go out to his field to water and work the soil with no confirmation of progress. That farmer knows that his crop is at work underground. Whatever will grow tall needs an amazing root system. That root system takes time to develop, so the farmer waits expectantly. When the shoot finally breaks ground, it grows exponentially reaching 80-90 feet in a few months. Just because we don't see what is happening does not mean nothing is growing. That farmer put a lot of confidence in the seed he planted. The farmer never dug it up to plant something less time consuming or neglected it. He continued to nourish it 365 days a year with no proof of growth for five long years. But he trusts the seed to produce. That should teach us to patiently wait for what God is doing in us.

When mankind was hopelessly bound by sin, Jesus, God's seed, lay dead in the ground too. Jesus our Lord lay, planted by the faith of the eternal Father, hidden in the grave. It looked like He was dead and gone; all hope was buried there in Him. Friday was painful, the waiting was agonizing, but Sunday was still coming!

Jesus was the seed when He was in the grave; He was making a way for us to come forth freely receiving His resureection life. **Ephesians 2:8 (KJV)** [8] *For by grace are ye saved through faith; and that not of yourselves: it is the gift of*

God: God had planted a seed; He was growing a gift of eternal life. God planned for a great harvest. You and I are part of that crop.

Hebrews 11:1 (KJV) [1] *Now faith is the substance of things hoped for, the evidence of things not seen.* Real faith sees it done without evidence. God takes the tiny seed of faith and speaks it into the heart and we are saved. The Lord Jesus is alive from the dead and those of us who really know that we are saved are living in Him.

God doesn't need much to work with. He can do anything with less and still get the glory. Consider the miraculous works that He did in Israel with the most unlikely leaders.

When Gideon was hiding from the Midianites in fear God spoke to him. **Judges 6:12-14 (KJV)** [12] *And the angel of the LORD appeared unto him, and said unto him, The LORD is with thee, thou mighty man of valour.* [13] *And Gideon said unto him, Oh my Lord, if the LORD be with us, why then is all this befallen us? and where be all his miracles which our fathers told us of, saying, Did not the LORD bring us up from Egypt? but now the LORD hath forsaken us, and delivered us into the hands of the Midianites.* [14] *And the LORD looked upon him, and said, Go in this thy might, and thou shalt save Israel from the hand of the Midianites: have not I sent thee?* God called him mighty and said go in this thy strength. What strength? His own confession had been that they appeared to have been deserted; that if God was for them they would not be enslaved to their enemies. He more or less asked, "Where is the God of our fathers?" Then God said, "I am with you and I am sending you." That was all that he needed.

God said it is enough that you know that I am sending you and that I have promised deliverance. Gideon knew that there was a vast host of fierce warriors waiting to oppose him. The Bible tells us there were five kings with strong armies allied with the Midianites; in addition they were joined by other nomadic tribes and robbers. They were described as swarms devouring the land and inhabitants before them. There was enormous opposition and God called out to this nobody and said you will lead this devastated, impoverished and fearful people to victory against all odds.

When Gideon put on the anointing like a mantle and called the tribes of Israel together, about 32,000 men showed up. That was nothing in comparison to their enemies. **Judges 7:2-8 (KJV)** *[2] And the LORD said unto Gideon, The people that are with thee are too many for me to give the Midianites into their hands, lest Israel vaunt themselves against me, saying, Mine own hand hath saved me. [3] Now therefore go to, proclaim in the ears of the people, saying, Whosoever is fearful and afraid, let him return and depart early from mount Gilead. And there returned of the people twenty and* *two thousand; and there remained ten thousand.* God told him to send home two thirds of the Army. So now the ones that are left are no longer afraid, but then the Lord speaks again. *⁴ And the LORD said unto Gideon, The people are yet too many; bring them down unto the water, and I will try them for thee there: and it shall be, that of whom I say unto thee, This shall go with thee, the same shall go with thee; and of whomsoever I say unto thee, This shall not go with thee, the same shall not go… ⁷ And the LORD said unto Gideon, By the three hundred men that lapped will I save you, and deliver the Midianites into thine hand: and let all the other people go every man unto his place. ⁸ So the people took victuals in their hand, and their trumpets: and he sent all the rest of Israel every man unto his tent, and retained those three hundred men: and the host of Midian was beneath him in the valley.*

God said in effect, "I can do more with less." The reduction of resources was necessary! But God, that is just 300 men against an army that covers the hills and valleys and is trained and equipped and has a track record of consistently defeating armies larger than Israel. Remember that during the flood, God took the whole population down to eight people. If He could repopulate the world with them, He could make 300 men victorious.

The Israelites who remained did not arm themselves with swords and spears. The scripture tells us they each had a trumpet and a clay jar with a flame inside. The trumpet is for sounding the battle cry and the light was to help them see and be seen. These two items were not offensive weapons, but they would be enough when used as God instructed. God built confidence into Gideon by sending him to listen to his enemy. **Judges 7:11-15 (NLT)** *[11] Listen to what the Midianites are saying, and you will be greatly encouraged. Then you will be eager to attack." So Gideon took Purah and went down to the edge of the enemy camp. [12] The armies of Midian, Amalek, and the people of the east had settled in the valley like a swarm of locusts. Their camels were like grains of sand on the seashore—too many to count! [13] Gideon crept up just as a man was telling his companion about a dream. The man said, "I had this dream, and in my dream a loaf of barley bread came tumbling down into the Midianite camp. It hit a tent, turned it over, and knocked it flat!"* Barley bread was coarse and cheap; it was what poor people ate. He was saying that something unexpected and insignificant was going to destroy the wealthy and strong. *[14] His companion answered, "Your dream can mean only one thing—God has given Gideon son of Joash, the Israelite, victory over Midian and all its allies!" [15] When Gideon heard the dream and its interpretation, he bowed in worship before the LORD. Then he returned to the Israelite camp and shouted, "Get up! For the LORD has given you* *victory over the Midianite hordes!"* He did not say God will give you victory. He said it is already done. He made it past tense because he could now see it as God did.

God gave Gideon the boldness and a plan of attack. He divided his tiny troop into three bands. Each took their horn and their clay pot in hand. They stood strategically on three ridges overlooking the vast army and when Gideon blew his trumpet and smashed his pot, they did the same thing. The sleeping armies awoke suddenly around midnight to see fire all around them and hearing what sounded like thousands of trumpets calling for more troops. They were so terrorized and traumatized that they started killing one another. Before long, the whole camp was emptied out. There among the corpses lay weapons and treasures and supplies that Israel needed. God not only removed the threat against them, but He made them victors and restored what the enemy had stolen from them with interest.

"Gideon armed each man in his token army with nothing more than a ram's horn and a clay jar with a torch in it. Could it be that was a prophetic picture of God's army? We march out to conquer the world armed only with the horn of salvation, our fragile clay bodies, and the indwelling light of God's presence leaking out through the cracks of our human brokenness." (Tenney p. 33)

I love a song that Jason Gray sings. It is titled; *The wound is where the light gets in.* It is through the wound of Jesus that the light can enter into us and it is through our weaknesses and failures that His light shines brightest. **II Corinthians 4:6-7 (KJV)** *⁶ For God, who commanded the light to shine out of darkness, hath shined in our hearts, to give the light of the knowledge of the glory of God in the face of Jesus Christ. ⁷ But we have this treasure in earthen vessels, that the excellency of the power may be of God, and not of us.* Through His wounded hands and feet we catch a glimpse of the cost of salvation and the amazing changes to mankind because of them. Then the same light that is in our Lord begins to radiate from our broken vessels so that the world will see Him.

God delights in taking the unexpected and unequipped and making something out of nothing. When the prophet Samuel came to Jesse's house to anoint a new king, David was such a zero that his dad didn't call him to the feast. It was as if he did not even remember him until the prophet had rejected all of his brothers and asked, "Don't you have anyone else?" Jesse never considered David as eligible to become a king. He worked as a shepherd. That was a poor man's job but God saw more than his father saw. God took that zero and mightily used him.

When Goliath reproached the whole army of Israel and mocked God, no mighty warrior stepped up to take him down. Saul stood a full foot taller than every man there, but he just sat in his tent, polishing his armor. A young shepherd was willing to stand against the giant that sent fear through every soldier. God reduced the whole of the army with swords and shields and armor down to one boy with a sling and a few smooth stones.

David came face to face with his destiny. They could have sent a soldier, but they were all crippled by fear, and soldiers depend upon their training and their weapons. This shepherd knew how to put his life on the line in front of an enemy and fight depending only on God. **I Samuel 17:45-47 (KJV)** *[45] Then said David to the Philistine, Thou comest to me with a sword, and with a spear, and with a shield: but I come to thee in the name of the LORD of hosts, the God of the armies of Israel, whom thou hast defied. [46] This day will the LORD deliver thee into mine hand; and I will smite thee, and take thine head from thee; and I will give the carcases of the host of the Philistines this day unto the fowls of the air, and to the wild beasts of the earth; that all the earth may know that there is a God in Israel.* David knew he had a covenant relationship with the all-powerful God who had delivered him from the lion and the bear. *[47] And all this assembly shall know that the LORD saveth not with sword and spear: for the battle is the LORD'S, and he will give you into our hands.*

God can do more with one man or woman who will walk in faith and obedience than all the well-educated and fully equipped of this world. When you feel like you aren't much for Him to work with, get ready for the power and presence of God to do what you think is impossible.

Starting With Zero

John 1:29 (KJV) *²⁹ The next day John seeth Jesus coming unto him, and saith, Behold the Lamb of God, which taketh away the sin of the world.*

The Blood Has Your Name On It

There is something special about having a personalized invitation or a handmade gift that is engraved with your name. I once watched a TV show where a man was trying to impress his wife by using a laser to engrave her name on a grain of sand. Unfortunately, after hours of work, he dropped it on the floor and could not find it.

God put your name on something too, something of great value. He put your name on the blood. There was specific blood shed for the hard cases, for the greatest sins and the most difficult sicknesses. While Jesus shed blood intentionally for the whole of humanity, there was some of that blood with your name on it. Some of it was for your salvation and your healing and your peace and if you do not apply that which was shed specifically for you then that blood was wasted. That bit of suffering and sacrifice would be in vain. His sacrifice must never be neglected. That blood was ordained to cover your need; spirit, soul and body were to be forever changed by the blood that fell. "From the beginning of God's dealings with man…the heart of God rejoiced in that blood. Our heart will never rest nor find salvation until we too learn to walk and glory in the power of that blood." (Murray p. 18)

When we saw the passion of the Christ I remember people asking me why Mary would take cloth and wipe up the blood of Jesus. One reason I believe that she would do that is that such holy blood could not be treated as common; it was not to be wasted, discarded or shed without effect or purpose. For us, the blood given in our stead and in our name has to be used. It has to be taken and accepted and applied to our need.

There was no other way, no other sacrifice that would have been enough. **Hebrews 9:22 (KJV)** [22] *And almost all things are by the law purged with blood; and without shedding of blood is no remission.* God said the only way to give life back to the spiritually dead was for a spiritually live man to be offered up. The only way for what was tainted by sin to be purified was through blood. For centuries God allowed man to use a type and a shadow of Jesus. All those years, lambs, and bulls were offered as tokens of what was to come. Every year when the Passover lamb was killed it was a picture of the coming Christ. But those animals continually offered, only reminded mankind that sin was serious and that God had a plan of redemption. There was a virtual river of blood poured out that could never remove the stain of sin from mankind. Those animal sacrifices pointed at the guilt of man, but the blood of Jesus would show His perfect removal of sin.

"The ultimate gift of the sacrifice of God the Son, who had already been given before time, was pictured and anticipated in the gift of the blood of animals in sacrifice. Apart from the determination in the heart of God to give His Son, animal sacrifices meant less than zero. The blood of animals could not take away sin, and God was affronted by sacrifices that were presented merely as a religious ritual." (Smith p. 102)

One time I heard Perry Stone preach about the sacrificial lambs brought to the temple. A lamb was offered for each family. Those lambs were chosen at birth, and had to be inspected by the priest to make sure they had no spot and flaws of any kind. In order to be sure that the lambs were not mixed up, each father put his family's name on it. They used a bronze tag or placard to show that this lamb represented the "Smith" family. When God offered up His lamb for the whole of His family, He too put His name on it. The sign above the dying Lord said, "Jesus of Nazareth, King of the Jews." It was written in Hebrew, Greek and Latin. From ancient times the Hebrew people took the first letter of each word and analyzed text to see if those first letters carried a hidden message. It was called a Tetragrammaton. In Hebrew the first letters from that sentence were YHVH. This was the common acronym for Yahweh or Jehovah, the unspeakably holy name of God. It was written in the Old Testament more than 6000 times. "By placing this inscription where he did, Pilate wrote the holy name of God above God's lamb! He was the final sacrifice hanging on the pole." (Stone p. 52) The scribes demanded that Pilate change it to say "Jesus said He was the King of the Jews." If they did that, the Tetragrammaton would differ greatly. The Jewish priests were appalled at the hidden message saying Jesus was God's lamb dying for all of us. It was God the Father in heaven claiming His Lamb. John had already called Jesus the Lamb of God. **John 1:29 (KJV)** [29] *The next day John seeth Jesus coming unto him, and saith, Behold the Lamb of God, which taketh away the sin of the world.* That word lamb is not just any from the flock, it is the word that meant the chosen lamb, set aside, raised and groomed to be the sacrifice. That placard on the cross was God signing His name to cover us, but our names were written in the blood. That is covenant; both parties clearly marked to show they agreed to the terms of the covenant.

Hebrews 9:11-14 (KJV) *[11] But Christ being come an high priest of good things to come, by a greater and more perfect tabernacle, not made with hands, that is to say, not of this building; [12] Neither by the blood of goats and calves, but by his own blood he entered in once into the holy place, having obtained eternal redemption for us. [13] For if the blood of bulls and of goats, and the ashes of an heifer sprinkling the unclean, sanctifieth to the purifying of the flesh: [14] How much more shall the blood of Christ, who through the eternal Spirit offered himself without spot to God, purge your conscience from dead works to serve the living God?* Mankind could go free, not because of anything man could do, but because God had made His own offering. With the dying of Jesus came the death of guilt and shame. Sin had lost its grip on mankind. There was no longer a death sentence on the human race. The price paid takes away all sense of unworthiness and we should no longer have a sin consciousness, but a redemption consciousness. **Romans 8:1 (KJV)** *[1] There is therefore now no condemnation to them which are in Christ Jesus, who walk not after the flesh, but after the Spirit.* "Through the power of the blood our fallen nature is prevented from exercising its power… The blood works with ceaseless power to keep the soul clean. A heart that lives under the full power of the blood is a clean heart, cleansed from a guilty conscience prepared to draw near with perfect freedom." (Murray p. 88)

God ripped the veil in the temple from top to bottom, saying the way is no longer barred. We can come right into the Holy of Holies, right into His presence and fellowship. "Understanding this, we more fully comprehend this is the age of grace. The blood of Christ is continually, perpetually making atonement for our sins. Christ's blood provided payment for access into the presence of God." (Stone 88) When we ask for forgiveness the Father looks to the blood on the altar. The blood that was shed in our name, and our faith, put a demand on the anointing and we receive the benefit of the sacrifice—forgiveness. We are free because we are identified with the shed blood of Jesus.

The sacrifice of Jesus on the cross was the greatest of all the blood covenants. There was never a covenant cut that did not name the parties involved and the terms of the agreement. If a covenant was valid, it had to be specific; it was purposeful. It was never generic. This covenant was between Jesus and the Father concerning you personally. He was redeeming your soul. "For God to make the new covenant, the representative—the God Man, Jesus—had to shed His blood in death and, rising out of death, bring us the blessings of the new covenant in the authority of His shed blood."

(Smith p. 99) He was paying for your sin and He was removing the power of everything that came from the root of sin. "He who gave His blood for us will surely, every moment impart it...trust Him to impart to you and to make effective in you all that He intended." (Murray p. 19)

I Peter 1:18-23 (KJV) *[18] Forasmuch as ye know that ye were not redeemed with corruptible things, as silver and gold, from your vain conversation received by tradition from your fathers; [19] But with the precious blood of Christ, as of a lamb without blemish and without spot: [20] Who verily was foreordained before the foundation of the world, but was manifest in these last times for you,[21] Who by him do believe in God, that raised him up from the dead, and gave him glory; that your faith and hope might be in God. [22] Seeing ye have purified your souls in obeying the truth through the Spirit unto unfeigned love of the brethren, see that ye love one another with a pure heart fervently: [23] Being born again, not of corruptible seed, but of incorruptible, by the word of God, which liveth and abideth forever.* The blood changed our destiny. It changed our future and it changed our very nature—that blood should powerfully change our thoughts and attitude and behavior.

There was not a drop that fell without need or without intent. Every drop has a name on it and has a need on it. There is cancer being cured, leukemia, deafness and blindness disappearing in the droplets that fell from His body. There was the soul being set free in what pooled at the foot of the cross. It was not some generic faceless mass of humanity that was washed clean; it was no face in a crowd that was thought of. It was personal, intentional, directed sacrifice. Each drop, each stripe upon His back was there to bring hope, deliverance, salvation and healing to you and to me.

That blood right there had my name on it. That blood was designated for me. That blood which was shed for my health and well-being must not be wasted. From the first drop that fell at the hands of angry soldiers hitting Him and plucking out His beard, to the last drop that slipped from His pierced side, there was a soul attached with a name and their own sins and sicknesses that must be eradicated in this world.

Revelation 5:9 (KJV) *⁹ And they sung a new song, saying, Thou art worthy to take the book, and to open the seals thereof: for thou wast slain, and hast redeemed us to God by thy blood out of every kindred, and tongue, and people, and nation;*

The God of all eternity reached through time and brought that blood that was needed and offered and given for and to you; you just accept that it was yours from the beginning. He never wanted any of the blood to be ignored. He never wanted any of the sin to be left in place. He did not want any of our body to be damaged and infirmed. He made a way; He paid the price in full for you, for me.

That blood has your name on it. When the President's security detail sees a potential attack, the agent assigned jumps in front of the intended victim and takes the bullet. That is what Jesus did for us. He got between you and the whip. He got between you and the nail. What should have been your suffering and your death was taken vicariously by Christ Jesus that you would never have to bear it. If He paid for it, why do we tolerate it? If He took it, why do we attach ourselves to the sin and failure as if they belong to us? We do not deserve forgiveness but He bought it and freely gives it.

The blood was poured out to remove every sickness and disease that would ever touch you. He paid for your heart and lungs to be whole. He made sure your bones would be strong. He took from within Him perfect wholeness and applied it to your sickness and your need. From within His perfect mind He poured out peace and soundness of mind to you.

We do not deserve healing or forgiveness, but He bought it. Since He did, then for us to adhere to sin as if it is ours and to claim possession of sickness and disease and failure and condemnation implies the blood was less than enough. I want you to know the blood was enough. Because that blood has your name on it you no longer deserve death and hell. Because that blood has your name on it you do not deserve to be sick. Disease is not yours; it does not belong to you. Jesus shed blood to set you free. The blood was enough; you are legally free. You are loved and accepted and healed.

The name of each of us is microscopically inscribed upon the blood that fell. God's blood, holy blood that filled the veins of Jesus, has our name on it. Now that we are saved, our blood also has His name on it.

God made His plan simple. If believed in the heart and spoken in faith, the simplest prayers change us for eternity. **Romans 10:8-11 (KJV)** *[8] But what saith it? The word is nigh thee, even in thy mouth, and in thy heart: that is, the word of faith, which we preach; [9] That if thou shalt confess with thy mouth the Lord Jesus, and shalt believe in thine heart that God hath raised him from the dead, thou shalt be saved. [10] For with the heart man believeth unto righteousness; and with the mouth confession is made unto salvation. [11] For the scripture saith, Whosoever believeth on him shall not be ashamed.* "One definition of confessing unto salvation means to agree with the covenant and to acknowledge the covenant! The blood of Jesus must be applied by confession. The blood of Christ is the most powerful substance in the universe." (Stone p. 113) Redemption was purchased by Jesus and offered to all of mankind. **I John 1:9 (KJV)** *⁹ If we confess our sins, he is faithful and just to forgive us our sins, and to cleanse us from all unrighteousness.*

"So Christ has died and in death has overcome sin, death and the devil and now lives in the power of an endless life. We are literally joined to Him, and His history becomes our history. His death is ours, so that Paul could say that he was crucified with Christ, even as His resurrection is ours and we walk in the power of that resurrection…We become partakers of the divine nature; we share His eternal life and become members of the Father's family." (Smith p. 216)

Revelation 12:11 (KJV) *¹¹ And they overcame him by the blood of the Lamb, and by the word of their testimony; and they loved not their lives unto the death.* Every believer down through time has to trust in that same blood. That blood is perpetually cleansing us and ministering to us. If I really believe, I place my confidence in Jesus being exactly who He said He was. That tiny seed of faith that I have as a gift, is now planted in Him. It produces something from nothing, and I reap eternal life. I am now free by the power of that same blood to live in Him and partake of His life—eternal life. I know it is true because my name is in the blood.

John 16:7 (KJV) *⁷ Nevertheless I tell you the truth; It is expedient for you that I go away: for if I go not away, the Comforter will not come unto you; but if I depart, I will send him unto you.*

Holy Oil in Clay Vessels

The disciples had walked with Jesus and seen Him do miracles. They had heard Him preach and teach things that were wonderful and made the Father God real to the masses. They had seen Him operate in a power far greater than anything known to man. Why would He say this? **John 16:7 (KJV)** *⁷ Nevertheless I tell you the truth; It is expedient for you that I go away: for if I go not away, the Comforter will not come unto you; but if I depart, I will send him unto you.* What or who could possibly be more to them? They did not understand. To be honest, most of this world still does not understand this comforter, this Spirit. "The Holy Spirit would be everything to them, even more than the physical Jesus had been. They would accomplish more under His direction and power than they had ever done in the time of Jesus." (Cymbala p. 16) Jesus had been with them, and had operated by the Holy Spirit right in front of them. But what they needed was the Spirit in them. Jesus had been near. This One, this third part of the trinity, was going to take up residence within believers. "While Christ's work on the cross, the shedding of His blood, was the only way to settle the problem of guilt, sin and condemnation, the coming of the promised Holy Spirit was God's way of changing human beings from the inside out." (Cymbala p. 16)

John 14:15-17 (KJV) *[15] If ye love me, keep my commandments. [16] And I will pray the Father, and he shall give you another Comforter, that he may abide with you for ever; [17] Even the Spirit of truth; whom the world cannot receive, because it seeth him not, neither knoweth him: but ye know him; for he dwelleth with you, and shall be in you.* This Comforter would be one who would take hold, together with the believer, against any force of evil. He would join in working with believers against all the effects of the fall. He would not work alone, but would be an indwelling power to allow the believer to do what only Jesus had been able to do to date.

The Holy Spirit has been symbolized by fire, water, oil and wind. He is the most mysterious member of the Godhead. He is the essence of God's creative forces, and the power infuser. He is the presence of God on earth today. He is the passion and fire within us to accomplish what we could never have done on our own. He is like lightning flashing through a blackened sky and He is the One who cradles us in our brokenness. This Holy Spirit is controversial and misunderstood. If allowed to have free reign in men, He fills and floods every part of their being, drawing them into unity with God. He is essential to everything spiritual and continually points to Jesus and the Father because the three are perfectly united. There is no competition between Him and Jesus. Each had a role to play; each was expressing the will and heart of the Father on earth. Jesus said this Spirit would come. Because He would indwell us, He would be more present with the disciples throughout time than Jesus was while in the flesh. He would lead and comfort and teach and empower believers.

The disciples had found a great truth. They knew the way of salvation. They knew the world was desperately in need of what they knew to be true. Jesus had to die to redeem mankind. Jesus was alive again from the dead. The Holy Spirit was so vital that Jesus said, "Do not even go out and proclaim the resurrection freely until He comes."

Luke 24:46-49 (KJV) *[46] And said unto them, Thus it is written, and thus it behoved Christ to suffer, and to rise from the dead the third day: [47] And that repentance and remission of sins should be* *preached in his name among all nations, beginning at Jerusalem. ⁴⁸ And ye are witnesses of these things. ⁴⁹ And, behold, I send the promise of my Father upon you: but tarry ye in the city of Jerusalem, until ye be endued with power from on high.* "The world is dying; people are without the gospel; these men have the message of life; they have seen Jesus in the flesh and walked with him for days on end, both before and after his death and resurrection—and yet he tells them to wait." (Cymbala p. 30) Jesus knew the opposition those simple fishermen would face, they could not do this without the Holy Spirit.

Acts 1: 8 (KJV) *⁸ But ye shall receive power, after that the Holy Ghost is come upon you: and ye shall be witnesses unto me both in Jerusalem, and in all Judaea, and in Samaria, and unto the uttermost part of the earth.* Jesus said to wait until they were indwelt, wait until they got their source and then they could change the world.

The message of the cross and the empty tomb is the fullness of redemption. Those men knew it was true. The disciples were both passionate and committed but they were still weak humans and they needed more than a message. They needed the Messenger!

Acts 2:1-4 (KJV) *¹ And when the day of Pentecost was fully come, they were all with one accord in one place. ² And suddenly there came a sound from heaven as of a rushing mighty wind, and* *it filled all the house where they were sitting.* ³ *And there appeared unto them cloven tongues like as of fire, and it sat upon each of them.* ⁴ *And they were all filled with the Holy Ghost...*

"Notice Jesus did not say wait for any certain manifestation: the flickering flames, the rushing wind, or the speaking in tongues. He pointed them to their need of receiving spiritual power. The thrust in the New Testament was always toward the power itself rather than any particular manifestations that came alongside the power...What the New Testament believers wanted most was to receive special ability from God, and any manifestations were unexpected side issues." (Cymbala p. 32) The evidence of the Holy Spirit was undeniable. The manifestations were outstanding but the power of His presence was even more dramatic.

Every man was changed when the Holy Spirit showed up. The same men who ran in fear became bold witnesses. None of those early Christians had any reputation as great speakers, or as religious men, most of them were poor and uneducated and yet these were the ones Jesus chose. "Jesus knew it would be almost impossible for them to depend on their human ability instead, they would have to reach out to His promise of power from on high." (Cymbala p. 39) They needed power and presence. They needed a right here, right now experience with God that would never fade into memory but was a life changing infusion of God. They needed a God inside. "Something supernatural came from heaven and invaded men and women on earth, changing them forever." (Cymbala p. 41)

Much to my surprise that is exactly what I needed too. I was saved for over eight years. I was in a good Baptist church. I was taught the scriptures about salvation. I know I was born again, and I studied more than most. Everyone I knew well followed me to salvation. It was not that I was such a great witness. I don't really remember either witnessing or inviting people to church, but my Aunt, my sisters, my friends came with me. Evidently they saw something in my life change. I was faithful in all I knew, but I was not totally satisfied inside. I wanted a more personal walk with the Lord.

Then we moved to a new city and we had to find a new church. That something that was missing was drawing me. It was not long until my new neighbor, Janet, invited me to visit her church, which later became my church. The difference was palpable; they had passion. There was a feeling in the air. They really worshipped. Their music was alive. There were people speaking in tongues and manifestations I didn't understand, but there was also something real and I wanted that. Shortly after that visit, Janet and I started a heated discussion about who the Holy Ghost is and what is or is not for the church today. I did a lot of digging in my Bible to support my arguments. I found out that the same Holy Spirit was available here and now. Janet invited me to a revival service. It was then that I was to encounter my own upper room experience. No flames, no wind, but He came and moved into my life. My hunger for the Word of God became insatiable. I had a new desire to read the Bible. I desperately wanted to pray, both in my own language and the tongues He gave me. The passion level turned way up. I grew more in the first six months at that Full Gospel church than in all the years up to that point. Since then, I have experienced the power and presence of God to heal and deliver from hopeless situations, afflictions and addictions. Praying and seeing manifestation in the lives of others is amazing. I have operated in most of the gifts of the Spirit as listed in Corinthians.

I Corinthians 12:4-11 (KJV) *[4] Now there are diversities of gifts, but the same Spirit. [5] And there are differences of administrations, but the same Lord. [6] And there are diversities of operations, but it is the same God which worketh all in all. [7] But the manifestation of the Spirit is given to every man to profit withal. [8] For to one is given by the Spirit the word of wisdom; to another the word of knowledge by the same Spirit; [9] To another faith by the same Spirit; to another the gifts of healing by* *the same Spirit;* [10] *To another the working of miracles; to another prophecy; to another discerning of spirits; to another divers kinds of tongues; to another the interpretation of tongues:* [11] *But all these worketh that one and the selfsame Spirit, dividing to every man severally as he will.* Every gift is used to minister to mankind in a way that will draw men to God and allow God to intervene in their brokenness. No manifestation of the Holy Ghost is for show, or for the sake of enjoyment or personal gain. Always know that it is God the Father and Jesus our Savior who are represented and honored where the Spirit is moving. I am strongly urging you to seek God, the giver and not the gifts. My passion is all about Him, not what is in His hand.

It is the same Holy Spirit that draws us unto salvation and teaches us the Word of God that fills believers. Yes, you did receive Him as part of the salvation package and no, that is not the baptism of the Spirit. He is the representative of God here and now and He is still drawing men to Jesus. I try to explain it like this. Water is water. The Holy Spirit moved in when you got saved, you can never receive a different Holy Spirit. But you can change the relationship. The water in your glass represents Him in you when you got saved. The only difference I can say in words that make any sense is that at the baptism of the Holy Spirit that glass got dropped into the ocean. When the water is in you and you are in the water—that is a total immersion. It is a oneness with the Spirit. That is what happened to me. He gained supremacy in our day to day walk. He became more powerful and as a side effect, so did I. The early church called it being filled with the Spirit. That meant something to them; it was the qualification for deacons. [See Acts 6:1-9]

I Peter 4:10-11 (KJV) *[10] As every man hath received the gift, even so minister the same one to another, as good stewards of the manifold grace of God. [11] If any man speak, let him speak as the oracles of God; if any man minister, let him do it as of the ability which God giveth: that God in all things may be glorified through Jesus Christ, to whom be praise and dominion for ever and ever. Amen.* Once endued with power from on high, I could witness and preach and teach effectively. Now I was able to not just talk about a historical Jesus that had changed me, but about a living Christ who was with me in essentially all of my endeavors.

The person of the Holy Spirit is powerful and accessible to all believers. "He is Christ without the limitations of the flesh and the material world. He can reveal what Christ could not speak. He has resources of power greater than those Christ could use, and he makes possible greater works." (Cymbala p. 19) The Holy Spirit is the Spirit of God manifest in multiple ways, to bring victory to His church. He comes to these frail clay pots and damaged vessels and He pours in His Holy Oil until we overflow with His goodness. I pray that you cry out for more of Him continually, and draw from His unceasing supply of power. **I John 4:4 (KJV)** *⁴ Ye are of God, little children, and have overcome them: because greater is he that is in you, than he that is in the world.*

Starting With Zero

Acts 4:13 (KJV) *¹³ Now when they saw the boldness of Peter and John, and perceived that they were unlearned and ignorant men, they marvelled; and they took knowledge of them, that they had been with Jesus.*

Not Nearly Enough

God started a church with no educated leaders, no building, no finances and no advertisement. He knew that we do not need the things of this world. The world looked at the ones who had trusted in Jesus and said that is not nearly enough, they can never do anything of consequence. The Jewish Sanhedrin decided to kill Jesus and watch the rest of His ministry team scatter. The world looked at the disciples and thought they were nothing, but the world was wrong. With our God even one or two believers becomes a powerful majority.

The followers of Jesus had only one thing going for them. They had received the revelation that Jesus was the Christ. **Matthew 16:15-18 (KJV)** *[15] He saith unto them, But whom say ye that I am? [16] And Simon Peter answered and said, Thou art the Christ, the Son of the living God. [17] And Jesus answered and said unto him, Blessed art thou, Simon Barjona: for flesh and blood hath not* *revealed it unto thee, but my Father which is in heaven. ⁱ⁸ And I say also unto thee, That thou art Peter, and upon this rock I will build my church; and the gates of hell shall not prevail against it.* That one powerful revelation from God would change the destiny of millions. A handful of fishermen, a tax collector and some women with some serious baggage were gathered together. This group of unlikely leaders had followed the Lord and seen Him condemned as a sinner and a criminal; they watched Him die on the cross. They had run in fear and hidden from the authorities. They were not much, but they had potential to change the world. They had failed before but they did not let their failures define them. Though they were weak and flawed they were exactly who God had chosen. They refused to let their moments of weakness steal their destiny or abort their mission. The Lord had risen from the dead, and these misfits knew He was alive. He told them to wait for power from on high and they simply obeyed.

Acts 2:1-13 (KJV) *¹ And when the day of Pentecost was fully come, they were all with one accord in one place. ² And suddenly there came a sound from heaven as of a rushing mighty wind, and it filled all the house where they were sitting. ³ And there appeared unto them cloven tongues like as of fire, and it sat upon each of them. ⁴ And they were all filled with the Holy Ghost, and began to speak* *with other tongues, as the Spirit gave them utterance. ⁵ And there were dwelling at Jerusalem Jews, devout men, out of every nation under heaven. ⁶ Now when this was noised abroad, the multitude came together, and were confounded, because that every man heard them speak in his own language. ⁷ And they were all amazed and marvelled, saying one to another, Behold, are not all these which speak Galilaeans? ⁸ And how hear we every man in our own tongue, wherein we were born... we do hear them speak in our tongues the wonderful works of God. ¹² And they were all amazed, and were in doubt, saying one to another, What meaneth this? ¹³ Others mocking said, These men are full of new wine.*

It is a comfort to me that out of all the men standing there that day the one who had most fervently denied knowing Jesus stood up to preach the first sermon. Our Father does on the job training and Peter was now following the lead of the Holy Spirit.

Acts 2:14-24 (KJV) *¹⁴ But Peter, standing up with the eleven, lifted up his voice, and said unto them, Ye men of Judaea, and all ye that dwell at Jerusalem, be this known unto you, and hearken to my words: ¹⁵ For these are not drunken, as ye suppose, seeing it is but the third hour of the day.* [9 am] *¹⁶ But this is that which was spoken by the prophet Joel; ¹⁷ And it shall come to pass in the last days, saith God, I will pour out of my Spirit upon all flesh: and your sons and your daughters shall prophesy, and your young men shall see visions,* *and your old men shall dream dreams:* [18] *And on my servants and on my handmaidens I will pour out in those days of my Spirit; and they shall prophesy:* [19] *And I will shew wonders in heaven above, and signs in the earth beneath; blood, and fire, and vapour of smoke:* [20] *The sun shall be turned into darkness, and the moon into blood, before that great and notable day of the Lord come:* [21] *And it shall come to pass, that whosoever shall call on the name of the Lord shall be saved.* [22] *Ye men of Israel, hear these words; Jesus of Nazareth, a man approved of God among you by miracles and wonders and signs, which God did by him in the midst of you, as ye yourselves also know:* [23] *Him, being delivered by the determinate counsel and foreknowledge of God, ye have taken, and by wicked hands have crucified and slain:* [24] *Whom God hath raised up, having loosed the pains of death: because it was not possible that he should be holden of it.* Those are powerful words Peter. Jesus is the Son of God, offered as a sacrifice for our sins and alive—resurrected from the dead. So that all of you can be saved. He used the Old Testament scriptures that they had heard and understood for years and applied them to the current situation so that they could see that it was God's plan to forgive sin and build a family of believers. That is how God built His church.

Acts 2:37-41 (KJV) [37] *Now when they heard this, they were pricked in their heart, and said unto Peter and to the rest of the apostles, Men and brethren, what shall we do?* [38] *Then Peter said unto them, Repent, and be baptized every one of you in the name of Jesus Christ for the remission of sins,* *and ye shall receive the gift of the Holy Ghost. ³⁹ For the promise is unto you, and to your children, and to all that are afar off, even as many as the Lord our God shall call. ⁴⁰ And with many other words did he testify and exhort, saying, Save yourselves from this untoward generation. ⁴¹ Then they that gladly received his word were baptized: and the same day there were added unto them about three thousand souls.*

Rome and all of its resources could not stop the church. The Jewish Sanhedrin could not keep the people away. Poverty and unemployment and rejection by their families and loved ones did not hold believers back from their faith. Every time the apostles were arrested and the church came under attack, the Holy Spirit showed up and the church held strong and grew in numbers. God did not choose the brilliant minded or the wealthy or powerful. He started with a few simple men and women who had little potential in the natural. On their own they were not enough, did not know enough. That did not stop God from building a church family that has stood the test of time for over 2000 years and has redeemed millions of souls. **Acts 4:13 (KJV)** *¹³ Now when they saw the boldness of Peter and John, and perceived that they were unlearned and ignorant men, they marvelled; and they took knowledge of them, that they had been with Jesus.* They were nobodies but they were in close contact with the Lord and that made them unstoppable.

"The work of God is not by might of men or by the power of men but by his Spirit. It is by Him the truth convicts and converts, sanctifies and saves. The philosophies of men fail, but the Word of God in the demonstration of the Spirit prevails. Our wants are many, and our faults innumerable, but they are all comprehended in our lack of the Holy Ghost. We want nothing but the fire." (Cymbala p. 18)

When God started the House of Victory, we did not have much either. Just a few believers and a man called of God to pastor us. Twelve years ago about 20 people met in a rented school cafeteria to worship. We wanted a church in a dark area, where our light would make a difference. The day we looked at our current building there was a drug deal on the back parking lot and a woman getting saved at the front door. We had found a building for the church, but the bank said that we did not have enough money or enough members to take on a bank loan. The church had not been established long enough to get approval. They said it was impossible the whole time they were getting the papers together. Less than 40 Christians remodeled a building that would hold about 200. Not many members, none of whom had any real money, but like the early church we knew the Lord was with us and had called us. The church simply believed,

Philippians 4:13 (KJV) *¹³ I can do all things through Christ which strengtheneth me.* God was and is faithful.

    We are still not filling up even half of that building, but in the past 12 years we have sowed more than $160,000 into the pour and needy. The House of Victory tithes and gives offerings out of everything that comes into the church. We call it the Gift that Keeps Giving. We get to minister to hundreds through our outreaches to children and the homeless and military members and missions. We have established a food pantry that gives to hundreds of people every month, and most of the cost of that food isn't even included in the Gift that Keeps Giving; people just bring it in. We have built six churches in India, and drilled a well in Africa and we have never missed a payment on that loan they said we could not afford. What I am saying is this; God can do much with little and He delights in doing great things against all odds. In the natural we are not nearly enough, but with God we are well supplied. If the food pantry is low, we go shopping and then someone from outside the church donates either cash or food. Once the local post office called to tell us they did a food drive, another time a library called and told us they had collected for us. We never asked for that. Once a woman looking for the large community food pantry came to us by "mistake" and we guided her there, she left us a check for $500 to bless our pantry. Another time we went to the mailbox and found an envelope stuffed full of twenties, no note just $1200 in cash. God is faithful to the faithful; whatever He puts in our hands we give freely to the needy. We might be small but we are blessed.

"The resources of the church are in the *supply of the* spirit" [Phil 1:19] (Cymbala p.18) He is the greatest need in our time. "We are currently living in the era of the Holy Spirit as we await the return of our Savior Jesus Christ. Our Lord is seated at the Father's right hand in heaven, but He has sent the promised Spirit so that, through His power, we can fulfill all of God's will, defeat every device of Satan, and extend the kingdom of Christ here on earth." (Cymbala p.19)

Philippians 4:19 (KJV) *[19] But my God shall supply all your need according to his riches in glory by Christ Jesus.* While we are on this earth, we can trust in the support and supply of God. He takes what is not nearly enough and makes an abundant supply that will more than meet the needs around us. He did it for the early church and He is still doing it today.

Starting With Zero

I Corinthians 1:27-29(KJV) [27] But God hath chosen the foolish things of the world to confound the wise; and God hath chosen the weak things of the world to confound the things which are mighty; [28] And base things of the world, and things which are despised, hath God chosen, *yea*, and things which are not, to bring to nought things that are: [29] That no flesh should glory in his presence.

Ground Zero

Ground zero is the place of origin, the beginning, the initial change. For us that place is the cross, or rather our awareness of it. It is a place of conflict and a place of decision, but it is also our place of greatest victory.

Just like the early church leaders, we are not finished when we are saved, but we have begun to allow the Lord to change us. "The unpleasant truth is that much of the work of character development takes place near what we might call our personal ground zero. Scientists coined this term around 1946 to describe the point at which a nuclear explosion occurs. I'm using it to refer to the center of origin of rapid, intense, or violent activity or change; the very beginning: square one." (Tenney p 24) In my lifetime ground zero also refers to the destruction of the World Trade Center that fell to a terrorist attack. It shook the world. 911 was the first time I remember being aware that enemies could attack my homeland.

God takes us to a place of radical change. He makes us see the importance of our spiritual rebirth. We are subjected to various life changing situations. At that point we can truly commit and follow the Lord. God chooses to use men to do His work and represent Him on the earth. He does not find the qualified to call, but qualifies those who are called.

I Corinthians 1:23-31 (KJV) *[23] But we preach Christ crucified, unto the Jews a stumblingblock, and unto the Greeks foolishness; [24] But unto them which are called, both Jews and Greeks, Christ the power of God, and the wisdom of God. [25] Because the foolishness of God is wiser than men; and the weakness of God is stronger than men. [26] For ye see your calling, brethren, how that not many wise men after the flesh, not many mighty, not many noble, are called: [27] But God hath chosen the foolish things of the world to confound the wise; and God hath chosen the weak things of the world to confound the things which are mighty; [28] And base things of the world, and things which are despised, hath God chosen, yea, and things which are not, to bring to nought things that are: [29] That no flesh should glory in his presence. [30] But of him are ye in Christ Jesus, who of God is made unto us wisdom, and righteousness, and sanctification, and redemption: [31] That, according as it is written, He that glorieth, let him glory in the Lord.*

He uses the imperfect men who say yes to salvation and to service. "The more inadequate you feel, the greater will be your potential role in the divine equation for this generation." (Tenney p 25) He reveals Himself to us, challenges us and changes us. Most of those changes are painful and some take years to complete. Some are rapid. God starts at conversion, the saving of the soul. That is the moment we see the Lord Jesus as our own Lord. It is the time when Jesus not only died for the world but it became personal—it was for me. It is when we stop living for self and begin living for Him.

"When Saul, the murdering religious fanatic, reached a low point on the Damascus road, it became a starting point for the high calling of his life. Thirty seconds in the manifest presence of God converted the murderer named Saul into the martyr named Paul. But he had to come to a personal ground zero. He referred to this rapid change for the rest of his heroic life. Ground zero has the potential to birth heroes." (Tenney p 25) That man who was killing Christians became the champion of the early church because he allowed his past failures to motivate him to work hard to display the power of the cross. He wrote 2/3 of the New Testament, mostly from within a jail cell. He was feared by other Christians, arrested, beaten, and denounced by most of society, but his weaknesses became his strengths.

God also used two murderers named David and Moses. He used prostitutes and barren women to birth a linage for Christ. Tommy Tenney says, "God prefers to invest His glory in the impossible and improbable because it is always clear that deity did it, and not the hand of flesh." (Tenney p 27) I know this, that all of the most powerful men of God

I have ever met are keenly aware that they are nothing without God.

My life wasn't so perfect either. My public disgrace came in the spring of 1971. I know how that woman caught in adultery felt. At seventeen I faced my parents and told them that I was pregnant. There was the same sense of worthlessness. The man who had asked me to marry him, told me to have an abortion. There was no mercy, no offer of grace, just that I got caught in my promiscuity and the undeniable truth that I was going to have a baby, alone, without support. I felt used and damaged, dirty and broken and rejected. I felt judged by almost everyone.

I felt like every other woman down through time caught in sexual failure and thrown at the feet of Jesus to be judged and condemned and to die in their sin. It was while I was carrying the child no one but me accepted or wanted that I first heard the gospel and that I could be saved. I prayed with a TV evangelist, but my decision was weak and my knowledge and faith were nonexistent so I cannot really say I was saved, but I opened the door a crack. God was not mad at me after all. Nothing seemed to change, except that maybe I was more open to forgiveness. I knew my sin, I loved my child, but I knew shame as well. I was not proud that I was carrying a child conceived in sin. Most of the time I was alone, and I dwelt on my failure and the rejection I felt. I had never considered aborting my baby and I was not giving my child up for adoption either. I had lost the man I loved, lost the respect of my parents and my friends, and I had placed my life on a very hard road. God had a plan to turn it all around. It was a ground zero for sure.

I met my husband during that time; he became my friend and later I fell in love with him. I married Buzz shortly after Marie was born. She was not his biologically, but he loved us both and the marriage softened the harshness I had lived in. Being loved and married made me feel like my sin was no longer on public display. That sin was still present with me, just less noticeable to others.

I was not really saved for almost another year, but when I openly admitted my guilt and looked up from my position in the dirt at the feet of Jesus, I saw only love and forgiveness. I heard all the stones of condemnation falling and with every thud, the echo of my Lord. *"Neither do I condemn thee: go, and sin no more."*

From that day forward I began to change. I read the Bible and served where I could in my church. I grew in understanding. I faced other challenges. My husband started drinking and nearly divorced me, my daughter nearly died; my health was stolen a few times. All of those were opportunities to draw nearer and trust in the Lord or to turn away. Fortunately, I chose His will over mine and all is well. I don't believe I would be as effective as a teacher, a minister or even an author without those times when my whole world seemed to blow up.

So where does your ground zero leave you? It leaves you with the chance to pick up the pieces of your broken life and allow the Lord to heal and to change you. You might be a zero or in a crisis so awful it feels like an explosion the size of Texas. This is the time to place the problem firmly in the Lord's hands and to take just one step at a time towards your destiny.

I Peter 5:6-7 (KJV) *⁶ Humble yourselves therefore under the mighty hand of God, that he may exalt you in due time: ⁷ Casting all your care upon him; for he careth for you.*

Matthew 25:14-15 (KJV) *¹⁴ For the kingdom of heaven is as a man travelling into a far country, who called his own servants, and delivered unto them his goods. ¹⁵ And unto one he gave five talents, to another two, and to another one; to every man according to his several ability; and straightway took his journey.* It's a long passage but suffice it to say the man who had five talents and he who had two both doubled the investment. They both got honored and entrusted with more responsibility.

Matthew 25:24-26 (KJV) *[24] Then he which had received the one talent came and said...[25] And I was afraid, and went and hid thy talent in the earth: lo, there thou hast that is thine. [26] His lord answered and said unto him, Thou wicked and slothful servant...* It was not about the money. The problem was that the man did not let God work through his lack to produce anything. His near nothing could have been his chance to come out of an internal image as a zero to become more. He was chastised because he did not let God do anything. "If all you have to sow into God's ground is your weakness, your pitiful praise, or a tiny seed of faith, then your zero may be enough to birth a miracle in your life! God is waiting for us to run to Him when we wake up at ground zero. One of the greatest opportunities we have to give Him glory is the day we discover we are helpless, hopeless and worthless unless He shows up." (Tenney p. 28) That man could have advanced his position in life, instead he refused to try.

You do not need to possess some unrealistic talent or belief; if you come with just a little bit of faith, you are going to receive your request. Sow the tiny seed of faith you have and your need will be met. A father with a desperate need came to the disciples while Jesus was away and asked for their help, but nothing changed. Then he cried out to Jesus for help. Jesus never said no; He did not rebuke him for his lack of faith. Jesus saw the man's inner struggle. He told the fearful father that his son's deliverance was possible. He asked the man to take just a tiny step of faith. You can openly admit your weakness and cry out like that father with the demon possessed son. "Help me in my unbelief." **Mark 9:22-24 (KJV)** *^{22} And ofttimes it hath cast him into the fire, and into the waters, to destroy him: but if thou canst do anything, have compassion on us, and help us. ^{23} Jesus said unto him, If thou canst believe, all things are possible to him that believeth.^{24} And straightway the father of the child cried out, and said with tears, Lord, I believe; help thou mine unbelief.* It is alright to say, "God help me in the area I have struggled to believe. Help me to see it as done. Help me in the areas where I let fear and doubt in. Help me to change. Help me to trust you with the whole of my being." He knows how to get you from this ground zero to victory.

God saved you so that you could do more than just say, 'I didn't lose faith and I made it to heaven." He sowed into your life enough for you to bring people with you. God wanted you to have real victory and an abundance to offer to the desperate people you meet. If you are in need, ask. Then rejoice in His provision. Where you are weak and empty let Him fill you. Plant the seeds of faith, and allow changes so He can best use you and the skills, talents and understanding He invests in you. Your ground zero just might be a tribute to His presence in your life.

John 20:27-29 (KJV) [27] Then saith he to Thomas, Reach hither thy finger, and behold my hands; and reach hither thy hand, and thrust *it* into my side: and be not faithless, but believing. [28] And Thomas answered and said unto him, My Lord and my God. [29] Jesus saith unto him, Thomas, because thou hast seen me, thou hast believed: blessed *are* they that have not seen, and *yet* have believed.

Looking Through the Nail Print

When my husband and I watched a nationally televised parade last year we commented on how differently our TV view was from those who were sitting along the parade route. We were trying to catch a glimpse of our grandson, Thomas, in the Marching 100 as they went along the route. I got one quick shot of him, but he wasn't up close and it only lasted a second. Yes, things were bigger than life to those standing on the road, but we saw through the lens of more than one camera and had a perspective that no one along that route could fully see. There was no tall person in the way, no horse that stood between us and the float behind him. There were no phone poles or signs or cars in our way; we could see a lot better than those people, but we still didn't see all of it at once, like God does.

Our problem is one of perspective. Like when you are on a plane and the houses and cars below seem tiny. The people in those houses don't feel small or think of you as big; to them you are just a tiny dot in the sky maybe even smaller than the birds in their yard. When we remember how big our God is, our problems shrink. We just have to get to where God lifts us up to His position where we can see clearly.

It isn't so important how this moment, this crisis, appears from here or from my vantage point as what does it look like from God's vantage point. If we could grasp it in the whole of time and in relation to the big picture, we would not worry.

Ephesians 2:4-7 (KJV) *^{4} But God, who is rich in mercy, for his great love wherewith he loved us, ^{5} Even when we were dead in sins, hath quickened us together with Christ, (by grace ye are saved;)* He saved us, He gave us life and that more abundant but not only that. He moved me positionally. He changed my viewpoint. *^{6} And hath raised us up together, and made us sit together in heavenly places in Christ Jesus: ^{7} That in the ages to come he might shew the exceeding riches of his grace in his kindness toward us through Christ Jesus.* The Bible tells us that God made man in His image and He has invited us to sit with Him in heavenly places. That is a position that allows us to see what only God could have seen. We can have that place of intimacy that lets us see beyond the here and now, beyond the hurt and pain. It places us above fear and negative reports. It lets us hear the facts and still know that He who is truth is much more powerful than any of those things.

We need to be seeing things the way He does, from God's perspective. When we look at it from His viewpoint, we recognize things are never quite as big and challenging as they seem from earth. He is not worried or fearful or even challenged by what is seen from His perspective. "You need more than an attitude adjustment; you need an altitude adjustment. You need to view circumstances as your heavenly Father sees them." (Tenney p. 4) His view is not obstructed by time or space or anything that blocks a perfect picture of the truth.

My Pastor always says look at the big picture. How huge is this in the fullness of eternity or even the overall picture of any one life? How much will it matter a year from now? What lens are you looking through? Are you looking through your fear or pain, or through your knowledge or past experience or through your natural vision? Are you looking with the eye of faith?

What if we looked through the nail print? What if we saw this in view of the whole of the sacrifice of Jesus? What if we looked at it knowing we were redeemed and loved to such a degree that He changes everything about us? What then?

His wound is our viewpoint. Everything has to be seen through the cost of salvation, the death of natural hope and the promise of resurrection. That hole in His hand is our magnifying glass. We see clearly when we see what God accomplished with that nail.

Isaiah 40:28-31 (KJV) *²⁸ Hast thou not known? hast thou not heard, that the everlasting God, the LORD, the Creator of the ends of the earth, fainteth not, neither is weary? there is no searching of his understanding. ²⁹ He giveth power to the faint; and to them that have no might he increaseth strength. ³⁰ Even the youths shall faint and be weary, and the young men shall utterly fall: ³¹ But they that wait upon the LORD shall renew their strength; they shall mount up with wings as eagles; they shall run, and not be weary; and they shall walk, and not faint.* Waiting on Him isn't just us sitting still for a long time. It means we serve Him like a waiter in a restaurant. We anticipate His next move, and are quick to respond to His call. We do not rush Him, neither do we cause delay. We watch Him closely. **Psalm 123:2 (KJV)** *² Behold, as the eyes of servants look unto the hand of their masters, and as the eyes of a maiden unto the hand of her mistress; so our eyes wait upon the LORD our God, until that he have mercy upon us.* Our waiting is active, not passive. We keep our focus on our Master continually. We are attentive, watching for direction.

We don't always have a smooth ride through life. We are faced with opposition. Sometimes it feels like our whole world is upside down and we don't know what to do. **Jeremiah 29:10-14 (KJV)** *[10] For thus saith the LORD, That after seventy years be accomplished at Babylon I will visit you, and perform my good word toward you, in causing you to return to this place.* The nation of Israel was taken into Babylon. They are prisoners of war, captives, and the man of God just told them you are going to stay here for 70 years before anything good happens. That is a lifetime. It is a long time to be in a different land and culture and subservient to their captors. Most of the men he prophesied to would die in that foreign land. They would suffer and after that, hope; after that the promise would manifest. *[11] For I know the thoughts that I think toward you, saith the LORD, thoughts of peace, and not of evil, to give you an expected end. [12] Then shall ye call upon me, and ye shall go and pray unto me, and I will hearken unto you. [13] And ye shall seek me, and find me, when ye shall search for me with all your heart. [4] And I will be found of you, saith the LORD: and I will turn away your captivity, and I will gather you from all the nations, and from all the places whither I have driven you, saith the*

LORD; *and I will bring you again into the place whence I caused you to be carried away captive.* God puts us in the middle of His purpose, on purpose. "He carefully plants us in places of destiny where our pain, our faith, and passion collide with His abundance, faithfulness and compassion. Everything you've longed for is already promised and paid for in full and perhaps it isn't delivered yet. Heaven's blood-certified check is in the mail." (Tenney p. 40)

God wants us dependent upon Him and confident in His ability when we face our biggest giants. God may not change your situation today, but He might be changing you and how you see it. We might be looking through the pain right now, but God sees the whole of how it will leave us and maybe a new path where He will lead us.

We all love miracles, but no one wants to desperately need one. The process is painful. The wait seems unbearable. The scenery is ugly, but that is what it takes to get to the miraculous. "The rugged territory between having enough and not having enough features the same geography as the place between already promised and not yet received. If it were up to us we would choose the easier path and live on one side or the other but it is not up to us." (Tenney p. 40) Sometimes that place where we are waiting out the promise and provision of God seems like it will last forever and our situation looks like a mountain range in front of us.

Luke 18:27 (KJV) *²⁷ And he said, The things which are impossible with men are possible with God.* If you have reached the place where everything is hopeless and impossible you are now eligible for a miracle and when you look through the nail print you will see that Jesus already paid for your perfect provision, and for your total healing and your comfort in the deepest and darkest of valleys. I remember when a friend found a lump under her arm and the doctors were running tests. Someone asked her what she was going to do. Her response was, "I get to trust God." She did not say I will have to trust Him. She did not say she was worried and fearful; she responded in faith and said it was a privilege to be able to go to her Father knowing that Jesus had obtained her healing. Weeks later, she got a good report, but while she waited she acted as if it had already been received. That is looking through the nail print.

If it were up to mankind, Lazarus would not have needed a resurrection. No leper would have needed to be made whole. If he had a choice the blind man would have been born seeing, but there is nothing to shout about in not needing a miracle. We all want to see the miraculous, but no one wants to suffer. God sometimes waits until all your efforts have led to failure. He lets our dead dream begin to rot in its grave before He does what is impossible to us, but then only He can receive the glory.

Matthew 14:23-32 (KJV) *^{23} And when he had sent the multitudes away, he went up into a mountain apart to pray: and when the evening was come, he was there alone. ^{24} But the ship was now in the midst of the sea, tossed with waves: for the wind was contrary.* Nothing happened until it felt like they were all alone, in the darkest part of the night, while a ship sinking, hurricane force storm raged. Sound familiar? THAT'S LIFE. *^{25} And in the fourth watch of the night Jesus went unto them, walking on the sea. ^{26} And when the disciples saw him walking on the sea, they were troubled, saying, It is a spirit; and they cried out for fear. ^{27} But straightway Jesus spake unto them, saying, Be of good cheer; it is I; be not afraid. ^{28} And Peter answered him and said, Lord, if it be thou, bid me come unto thee on the water. ^{29} And he said, Come. And when Peter was come down out of the ship, he walked on the water, to go to Jesus. ^{30} But when he saw the wind boisterous, he was afraid; and beginning to sink, he cried, saying, Lord, save me. ^{31} And immediately Jesus stretched forth his hand, and caught him, and said unto him, O thou of little faith, wherefore didst thou doubt? ^{32} And when they were come into the ship, the wind ceased.* Once Peter is on the water he has to keep looking at Jesus if he plans to stay afloat. You are either looking at Jesus or you are not. You cannot be both looking at the Lord and looking fearfully at your problem and focusing on what can go wrong. You are either focused on your need or on the One who died for that need to be met. Look at that nail print in His hand He put it there for you.

The print of the nail is a reminder that we have a covenant with God. "Our Lord confirmed the teaching of the Old Testament offerings—that man can live only through the death of another, thus obtaining a life that through resurrection has become eternal." (Murray p. 14) That nail hole says we are redeemed. Jesus died as our substitute and identified as our sacrifice. His blood was full payment for our salvation and all sin. His blood covered every need we would ever have. Jesus also rose victorious over all sin and death. He rose to eternal life and gave it to us. That permanent mark on the body of the Lord makes sure we are always before His eyes and we are always made righteous and declared pure by means of His suffering.

Heaven is forever marked with your image. The payment for your sin and healing is right there. **Isaiah 49:16 (KJV)** *^{16} Behold, I have graven thee upon the palms of my hands;* God marked Himself in covenant with you, and every time He looks at those hands He sees forgiveness, deliverance, provision and healing. God sees the finished work of the Cross. Look at what He sees and you will see yourself free.

Even John had a hard time seeing everything the way it looks from God's perspective. **Revelation 5:4-6 (KJV)** *[4] And I wept much, because no man was found worthy to open and to read the book, neither to look thereon. [5] And one of the elders saith unto me, Weep not: behold, the Lion of the tribe of Juda, the Root of David, hath prevailed to open the book, and to loose the seven seals thereof. [6] And I beheld, and, lo, in the midst of the throne and of the four beasts, and in the midst of the elders, stood a Lamb as it had been slain, having seven horns and seven eyes, which are the seven Spirits of God sent forth into all the earth.* John did not see a lion. He saw the Lamb, but the angel saw a lion. The difference was John needed a sacrificial Lamb to die for him and the angel had a heavenly perspective; he saw the Lion of the Tribe of Judah. Jesus is both, but our attitude is dependent upon our perspective. We need to see things from God's viewpoint. Jesus is powerful; the nail print shows He has conquered sin and death. He is not a victim; He is the victor. He did not succumb to death, but defeated it and He is more than able to meet our every need.

Keep looking until you see the problem through that hole in His wrist and you will see it is already covered by the blood. If the problem is still large, it is because you are seeing it from this side, not from God's side. You can be weary and wailing if your eye is on the problem or you can be worshipping because your eye is on the Solution.

You don't want the reputation of Thomas. **John 20:25-29 (KJV)** *[25] The other disciples therefore said unto him, We have seen the Lord. But he said unto them, Except I shall see in his hands the print of the nails, and put my finger into the print of the nails, and thrust my hand into his side, I will not believe.* Faith and doubt are both taken by choice. Thomas never said I cannot believe but he boldly said I will not. *[26] And after eight days again his disciples were within, and Thomas with them: then came Jesus, the doors being shut, and stood in the midst, and said, Peace be unto you. [27] Then saith he to Thomas, Reach hither thy finger, and behold my hands; and reach hither thy hand, and thrust it into my side: and be not faithless, but believing. [28] And Thomas answered and said unto him, My Lord and my God. [29] Jesus saith unto him, Thomas, because thou hast seen me, thou hast believed: blessed are they that have not seen, and yet have believed.* None of us was there to see His hand outstretched on the cross. We did not see Jesus extend His hand to Thomas as proof of the resurrection. We believe by choice. We are blessed to be able to believe.

"Invest all that you have and all that you are in the One who was buried, the One who rose, and the One and only who ascended on high to sit at the right hand of the Father." (Tenney p.7) See this problem in proportion to His provision. Look through the lens of faith. You cannot see defeat or fear death while looking through the nail print.

The same hand that stretched out on the cross to pay for your sin and overcome death, hell and the grave is upon you to insure your victory. Are you looking through that place? Do you not know that everything that opposed Him is now weak and impotent and He is alive? Change your perspective. Get your eyes back on the One who comes walking on water to get to you if need be. Remember you have a covenant with God. He is on your side. You are His beloved, blood bought, child. You are guaranteed a victory.

You aren't a doubting Thomas who has to see to believe or touch the hole in His wrist. Just adjust your perspective so that you can see this time in your life through that nail print; it will look a lot different.

Starting With Zero

Rev. Kathryn L. Smith

II Kings 4:2 (KJV) *² And Elisha said unto her, What shall I do for thee? tell me, what hast thou in the house?*

What is in Your Hand?

Have you ever watched MacGyver? He takes a little of this and a little of that and creates something incredible. Maybe He knows something of Bible principles. He always just looks around to see what is available and once he knows what he has to work with, he makes a solution to the problem. If he has pocket knife, a gum wrapper or a can of hairspray there will be a way out of his predicament. I saw a show one time where he made a smoke screen out of flour and baking soda. He once made a Geiger counter out of a radio and a cell phone. That man totally understands the principal of starting with very little and ending up with whatever is needed.

Acting in desperation is better than falling into despair. God is not concerned with what you don't have—your lack; He is ready to use what you do have. What is it that you have in your hand?

II Kings 4:1-7 (KJV) *[1] Now there cried a certain woman of the wives of the sons of the* *prophets unto Elisha, saying, Thy servant my husband is dead; and thou knowest that thy servant did fear the LORD: and the creditor is come to take unto him my two sons to be bondmen. [2] And Elisha said unto her, What shall I do for thee? tell me, what hast thou in the house?* What do you have? Not a rejection or a comment about the size of her problem. The prophet did not say, "Oh that's a great need." Notice he did not say, "Just deal with it." He did not respond in fear. He asked her, "What do you have?" God always supplies what we need and uses what we have out of that supply. *And she said, Thine handmaid hath not anything in the house, save a pot of oil. [3] Then he said, Go, borrow thee vessels abroad of all thy neighbors, even empty vessels; borrow not a few. [4] And when thou art come in, thou shalt shut the door upon thee and upon thy sons, and shalt pour out into all those vessels, and thou shalt set aside that which is full. [5] So she went from him, and shut the door upon her and upon her sons, who brought the vessels to her; and she poured out. [6] And it came to pass, when the vessels were full, that she said unto her son, Bring me yet a vessel. And he said unto her, There is not a vessel more. And the oil stayed. [7] Then she came and told the man of God. And he said, Go, sell the oil, and pay thy debt, and live thou and thy children of the rest.* God is the great I Am, the One who supplies all our needs. He made sure she had a tiny bit of oil to start with. He sent her to a man of faith. He showed her how to use faith to multiply her supply. He did not just get her out of debt, but also gave her an income to live on.

God's supernatural supply was more than enough for her need. God did not rain down money on her, He had her use what was in her hand and then He multiplied it like the fish and loaves that fed the multitudes. If she stayed in worry and fear and did nothing she would have lost both her sons and she would have likely starved to death.

God knows how to take care of poor widows and the prophets who carry His word as well. That was not the first time God made an abundance of oil to meet a desperate need. When Elijah was in hiding during the years of drought, God sent him to drink from the brook and had the raven feed him every day morning and evening, but eventually the brook dried up. **I Kings 17:8-16 (KJV)** *[8] And the word of the LORD came unto him, saying, [9] Arise, get thee to Zarephath, which belongeth to Zidon, and dwell there: behold, I have commanded a widow woman there to sustain thee.* Widows were generally poor, and women during this time did not have any job opportunities. It was an act of faith to think some foreign widow could feed him, but Elijah went. *[10] So he arose and went to Zarephath. And when he came to the gate of the city, behold, the widow woman was there gathering of sticks: and he called to her, and said, Fetch me, I pray thee, a little water in a vessel, that I may drink. [11] And as she was going to fetch it, he called to her, and said, Bring me, I pray thee, a morsel of bread in thine hand. [12] And she said, As the LORD thy God liveth, I have not a cake, but an handful of meal in a barrel, and a little oil in a cruse: and, behold, I am gathering two sticks, that I may go in and dress it* *for me and my son, that we may eat it, and die.* ^{13} *And Elijah said unto her, Fear not; go and do as thou hast said: but make me thereof a little cake first, and bring it unto me, and after make for thee and for thy son.* ^{14} *For thus saith the LORD God of Israel, The barrel of meal shall not waste, neither shall the cruse of oil fail, until the day that the LORD sendeth rain upon the earth.* ^{15} *And she went and did according to the saying of Elijah: and she, and he, and her house, did eat many days.* ^{16} *And the barrel of meal wasted not, neither did the cruse of oil fail, according to the word of the LORD, which he spake by Elijah.* That is the same kind of supernatural increase of supply as the oil in the previous scripture. God did not start with nothing but in each case He took what He had already put in their hand and used it to create a supernatural supply until the need was gone.

Some had nothing more than a bit of faith, but it was enough when invested in the Lord to meet their total need. The woman with the issue of blood said if I can just get to Him I will reach out and take hold of the miracle, I will be healed. She did, and she was. Blind Bartimaeus had enough faith to shout, *"Son of David have mercy on me."* Both of them spent years in their affliction and their need was great but what they had in them was enough to get them out of distress and into victory.

Colossians 2:6-7 (KJV) ^{6} *As ye have therefore received Christ Jesus the Lord, so walk ye* *in him:* ⁷ *Rooted and built up in him, and stablished in the faith, as ye have been taught, abounding therein with thanksgiving.* Take what God has placed in you and in your hand and use it. Act upon your faith. Trust and speak. Believe and move forward. Do something with what He has entrusted to you.

What do you have in your hand? What can you use to get the job done? Surely, God has not left you with nothing to offer and no way out. I remember a pastor who had huge medical bills. His wife had been ill and was now healed, but they were left seriously in debt. He did not want to file bankruptcy, and so he went to his creditors and told them, "Give me some time and I will find a way to repay all of it." He had a job that paid their regular bills, but this was above anything that income could provide, so he prayed for a way out and God sent him to people who needed their houses painted. Every week on his day off, he put on old clothes and climbed ladders to paint away his debt. That may not seem supernatural to you but God gave him the skill and the strength and enough customers to whittle down that mountain of debt. He never had to advertise and there was always another job lined up as he finished the house he was painting.

God will bless what you have put your hand to. I learned sign language at church, but years later God used it to pay my bills. As an interpreter, I had a lot of interesting experiences and I had a steady income. Twice, the Lord told professional fishermen who had caught nothing where to cast their nets and both times they nearly sunk their boats with the haul they brought in. [See Luke 5 and John 21] God always puts something in your hand, so that you are never left without support.

Matthew 17:24-27 (KJV) *^{24} And when they were come to Capernaum, they that received tribute money came to Peter, and said, Doth not your master pay tribute?* The tax collector was demanding payment. Peter was concerned and Jesus gave him an answer. There is no need to panic when you need money. Peter was a fisherman by trade before he became a disciple so Jesus used what was already in his skill set to meet the need. *^{27} Notwithstanding, lest we should offend them, go thou to the sea, and cast an hook, and take up the fish that first cometh up; and when thou hast opened his mouth, thou shalt find a piece of money: that take, and give unto them for me and thee.* When Peter listened to the Lord's command and obeyed, the provision appeared.

I remember a sermon from years ago when evangelist Bob Prettyman preached in a local church. His title was *What You Gonna Do With What You Got?* God never demands of us what we do not have. He does not ask for us to step out in faith on thin air, but He does expect us to use what is available to us. He told us about David who only had a sling and some small stones when he faced his destiny. He mentioned others who took the little they had and added to it faith and God made it more than enough. In those days, I did not have much money to put in the offering, but I have always been able to sew. That night I went home and made a pillowcase doll for the man's wife. I took it to her the next night and told her what I had was a talent and some materials and she told me she had been admiring a doll almost exactly like that at a craft show. God knew she would like it and impressed me to use what I had to bless both of us.

He gave the widow flour and oil. He gave a net busting catch of fish to exhausted fishermen. He provided a fish full of tax money for Peter. He has it all worked out. He has you positioned to get all that you need. All Jesus is asking is that you use what is in your hand.

Genesis 14:18-19 (KJV) [18] *And Melchizedek king of Salem brought forth bread and wine: and he was the priest of the most high God.* [19] *And he blessed him, and said, Blessed be Abram of the most high God, possessor of heaven and earth:*

Making Bread and Wine

Bread and wine were the staples of life, and they were always used when sacred feasts took place. It was bread and wine that Melchizedek brought to Abraham after he had rescued the small band that would become the nation of Israel. Naturally as Christians, we think of communion as well. Bread and wine represent the body and blood of our Lord Jesus and our relationship with Him.

In Biblical times, natural bread was eaten every day and wine was offered with meals because it was safer to drink than most of their water. There were women kneading bread everywhere the disciples looked. We are not talking about that kind of everyday bread making.

When Jesus was in the wilderness being tempted by the devil, the suggestion was "You are hungry by now. If you are the Son of God, just make these stones into bread." Jesus would not comply, He had nothing to prove and He would never give in to temptation. **Matthew 4:1-4 (KJV)**

¹ Then was Jesus led up of the Spirit into the wilderness to be tempted of the devil.² And when he had fasted forty days and forty nights, he was afterward an hungred. ³ And when the tempter came to him, he said, If thou be the Son of God, command that these stones be made bread. ⁴ But he answered and said, It is written, Man shall not live by bread alone, but by every word that proceedeth out of the mouth of God.

Had it not been a real possibility to change stones to bread, the devil would not have suggested it. If Jesus was not really hungry and capable it would not have even been a test. Both of those criteria were met. Jesus was both the Son of God with the ability to do creative miracles and He was fully human and required food to maintain health.

The devil is trying the same temptations he used against the first Adam, but Jesus would not bite. To Eve he said, "Has God said…" and to Jesus he says "Are you really the Son of God?" Both times his words were spoken to sow seeds of doubt and both times it was an offer to prove how independent they were. In both cases, the temptation involved satisfying natural hunger. "Intrinsically there was nothing wrong in Jesus performing a miracle to provide Himself with needed food. But to obey Satan is sin. Furthermore, Christ had come to share our humanity with us. He refused to use any power not at our disposal. He would not do anything that would be a denial of His incarnation." (Beacon vol. 6 p. 89) Jesus would never be forced to prove who He was; neither would He do what was permissible for His own physical comfort. **Matthew 4: 4 (KJV)** *⁴ But he answered and said, It is written, Man shall not live by bread alone, but by every word that proceedeth out of the mouth of God.* Jesus answered with scripture. It has been written and the Word stands true even now. We resist the enemy the same way.

More than three years later Jesus might very well have turned stones to bread. Jesus was crucified and resurrected and His disciples were a little unsure of what to expect next. It was very natural for them to return to their former occupation rather than sit idle until they got further instructions.

John 21:3-12 (KJV) *³ Simon Peter saith unto them, I go a fishing.* They spent the night fishing, without a catch to show for it and in the morning they saw Jesus on the shore and when He called to them, they came to the breakfast He had prepared. *⁹ As soon then as they were come to land, they saw a fire of coals there, and fish laid thereon, and bread.... ¹² Jesus saith unto them, Come and dine. And none of the disciples durst ask him, Who art thou? knowing that it was the Lord.* I do not think that Jesus went to a store and got them bread or fish. The fish were probably from the sea right there. If He wanted to, Jesus could command them to swim to shore and just pick them up with His hands. Bread was there too. I think this time when there was no temptation involved and the devil was already defeated, Jesus did just turn the stones to bread for the men He loved. It does not seem much of a stretch for the One who is the Bread of Life to provide them with supernatural bread. According to John, this was the third time Jesus revealed Himself to them after the resurrection. He had always presided as the leader and host at their meals, and here He was again handing them bread and fish and sharing in divine fellowship with these who had been His friends and would become His legacy. He fed them a simple meal, by means of a creative miracle, before sending them out to proclaim the gospel.

Looking back a few years, we see the first creative miracle of Jesus: the turning of water into wine. **John 2:1-11 (KJV)** *[1] And the third day there was a marriage in Cana of Galilee; and the mother of Jesus was there:* Mary is not mentioned by name; she may very well have been a member of this family, and she was most defiantly involved in the serving. That relationship explains why she and Jesus were called to the wedding. *[2] And both Jesus* *was called, and his disciples, to the marriage.³ And when they wanted wine, the mother of Jesus saith unto him, They have no wine.⁴ Jesus saith unto her, Woman, what have I to do with thee? mine hour is not yet come.* First of all, it is important to realize that for the Jewish people wedding feasts lasted for seven days. It was important for the family that they fully provide for their guest for the duration of that time. The feast was proof that the groom would be able to care for a family. If they did not have enough of anything it would have been an embarrassment; but the most important element of the feast was the wine. It was a horrible thing that the wine ran out. "This amounted to a social catastrophe for the families of the bride and groom. There is a Jewish saying, that without wine there is no joy," (Beacon vol. 7 p. 45) She was looking at her son to meet a need. I am sure He had provided for her since the death of Joseph. It is not clear that she expected a miracle, but she appears to have asked just that. She also may have been simply thinking they could help in the natural, but that is less likely. He called her "Woman." That sounds harsh to our ears, but none of His answer was harsh. It was a term of endearment during this time. Jesus also said *"what have I to do with thee? mine hour is not yet come."* This comment amounted to something like your viewpoint is natural, but mine is spiritual; we don't see the same things. She was making a demand on the anointing that Jesus carried. The need was natural, earthly, but because of her relationship, she appears to have dared to ask for a divine intervention. His purpose was not to meet their needs. She was asking Jesus to use His power for less than His intended purpose. He was functioning in the supernatural, and she needed to see that. She needed to understand that His mission was not for the comfort and provision of men but for the redemption of men. But since He was her son, Jesus was inclined to be a blessing to her and to those she loved. He had not verbally agreed to help, but she knew her son's heart. *⁵ His mother saith unto the servants, Whatsoever he saith unto you, do it.* In the margin of my Bible I have written, "Best advice ever given." *⁶ And there were set there six waterpots of stone, after the manner of the purifying of the Jews, containing two or three firkins apiece. ⁷ Jesus saith unto them, Fill the waterpots with water. And they filled them up to the brim. ⁸ And he saith unto them, Draw out now, and bear unto the governor of the feast. And they bare it. ⁹ When the ruler of the feast had tasted the water that was made wine, and knew not whence it was: (but the servants which drew the water knew;) the governor of the feast called the bridegroom, ¹⁰ And saith unto him, Every man at the beginning doth set forth good wine; and when men have well drunk, then that which is worse: but thou hast kept the good wine until now. ⁱⁱ This beginning of miracles did Jesus in Cana of Galilee, and manifested forth his glory; and his disciples believed on him.*

Jesus provided 120 gallons of wine which should be more than enough to satisfy all of the people throughout the rest of the celebration. He started with jars that were mostly empty. They had been used to provide the water that the guests used to wash their feet. "It is not accidental that John tells of their function as related to the manner of purifying of the Jews. For these vessels represent the whole way of the Law, legalism, which is shown to be inadequate for the real needs of man, and limited in comparison with the full scope and abundant joy of the gospel as symbolized by wine in such large quantity, and less than God's best for man. The old legal religion lacks wine, all the life energy is gone from it." (Beacon vol. 7 p. 46) The servants had to go and draw a great deal of water; their effort was proof of their faith. If they believed it would still be water when they drew it out, they would never have offered it to the one in charge of the feast.

There has been a lot of controversy over the question as to whether or not the wine had alcohol content. Let me just say this. Anything made from the fruit of the grape vine would have been translated as wine. Not only that but we must understand that the times were different. "Most of the grape juice was made into wine. This was done not simply for pleasure; it was a necessity. The water was unsafe for drinking unless it came from a fresh spring, and the milk supply was limited. When Paul told Timothy that he should drink a little wine for his stomach's sake, it was not necessarily because the wine would do his stomach good, but because the water might do it harm [I Tim 5:23]" (Gower p.109) Making natural wine requires a fermenting, or rotting process that lasted for a minimum of six weeks and I just don't see that as something that the Lord's wine contained. The people raved at the taste, so I am sure it was delicious. It was probably a premium juice. What had been scarce was now in abundant supply. "At its best, the Law was *a shadow of good things to come* Heb. 10:1; but now in Jesus Christ, the good things have come, available to all men, adequate for man's deepest needs. It is evident that Man's disappointment is God's appointment. Man's insufficiency is met by divine adequacy. Sorrow is turned to joy, and man's own shabby resources are supplanted by God's best." (Beacon vol. 7 p. 47) Jesus met their natural need but He also revealed a little of His glory and it helped the disciples to believe in Him.

Jesus will supply our every need. Most of the time, He does that through very ordinary means, but if need be He will do the miraculous for those who will both believe and obey Him. **Matthew 21:22 (KJV)** [22] *And all things, whatsoever ye shall ask in prayer, believing, ye shall receive.* Trust in Him and let Him provide for you and remember that excellent advice from the mother of our Lord. *Whatsoever he saith unto you, do it.*

Matthew 4:18-20 (KJV) *[18] And Jesus, walking by the sea of Galilee, saw two brethren, Simon called Peter, and Andrew his brother, casting a net into the sea: for they were fishers. [19] And he saith unto them, Follow me, and I will make you fishers of men. [20] And they straightway left their nets, and followed him.*

Fishing with Jesus

When I was young I loved to go fishing with my dad. It was rare that either of my sisters would get up, during a camping trip, at five in the morning to go out in the boat and sit quietly on the lake, but I loved that time alone with him. It was peaceful and it really did not matter if we caught many fish. It was just time well spent in nature with my dad. That wasn't the case for Peter, James or John. They were professional fishermen and the livelihood of their families depended upon a good catch.

Luke 5:1-11 (KJV) *[1] And it came to pass, that, as the people pressed upon him to hear the word of God, he stood by the lake of Gennesaret, [2] And saw two ships standing by the lake: but the fishermen were gone out of them, and were washing their nets. [3] And he entered into one of the ships, which was Simon's, and prayed him that he would thrust out a little from the land. And he sat down, and taught the people out of the ship. [4] Now when he had left speaking, he said unto Simon, Launch out into the deep, and let down your nets for a draught. [5] And Simon answering said unto him, Master, we have toiled all the night, and have taken* *nothing: nevertheless at thy word I will let down the net.* They knew these waters. Night was the best time to catch fish and they had nothing to show for an entire night of effort. Peter was saying that there was no use in trying anymore, but if the Lord said to do it, he would submit. *⁶ And when they had this done, they enclosed a great multitude of fishes: and their net brake. ⁷ And they beckoned unto their partners, which were in the other ship, that they should come and help them. And they came, and filled both the ships, so that they began to sink. ⁸ When Simon Peter saw it, he fell down at Jesus' knees, saying, Depart from me; for I am a sinful man, O Lord. ⁹ For he was astonished, and all that were with him, at the draught of the fishes which they had taken: ¹⁰ And so was also James, and John, the sons of Zebedee, which were partners with Simon. And Jesus said unto Simon, Fear not; from henceforth thou shalt catch men. ¹¹ And when they had brought their ships to land, they forsook all, and followed him.* Jesus called out a crew of poor, dirty, uneducated fishermen to create what would become His church. He proved His power by providing more than they could have ever imagined. Fishing with Jesus was a guaranteed net breaking catch.

Those very common fishermen followed Jesus and saw the miracles. They listened to Him speak and they knew Him well. They had a part in His anointing and ministry. And then they watched Jesus die a criminal's death at the hands of the Romans and the Jewish leaders. They knew joy and sorrow. They heard Mary say He was alive again.

Then the Lord had shown them the scars on His hands and feet. They knew the resurrection to be reality but they did not know how to proceed so they sat with their life on pause. Their future was undefined, and their destiny delayed. They did not have a plan of action. While they awaited further instructions from the Lord, they did what was normal for them, they went fishing.

John 21:3-12 (KJV) *³ Simon Peter saith unto them, I go a fishing.* Until I know what else to do, I will do what I do know how to do. *They say unto him, We also go with thee. They went forth, and entered into a ship immediately; and that night they caught nothing.* That sounds just like the first time they met Him. *⁴ But when the morning was now come, Jesus stood on the shore: but the disciples knew not that it was Jesus.* Maybe the shore was too far away for them to see Jesus clearly. It could be that like the men on the road to Emmaus, they were unaccustomed to seeing Him like this and they did not recognize Him. He chose to let them discover who He was in their own time. *⁵ Then Jesus saith unto them, Children, have ye any meat? They answered him, No. ⁶ And he said unto them, Cast the net on the right side of the ship, and ye shall find. They cast therefore, and now they were not able to draw it for the multitude of fish. ⁷ Therefore that disciple whom Jesus loved saith unto Peter, It is the Lord.* It was so clear to John, the same situation, the same kind of catch, this must be the Jesus. *Now when Simon Peter heard that it was the Lord, he girt his fisher's coat unto him, (for he was naked,)* Peter was not really naked, just shirtless, like a lot of men when they are working. *and did cast himself into the sea.* Just like the time he had walked on the water, Peter wanted to be near the Lord. If it meant getting wet it was better than waiting. So he dove in, swimming toward the shore and the Master he loved. *[8] And the other disciples came in a little ship; (for they were not far from land, but as it were two hundred cubits,) dragging the net with fishes. [9] As soon then as they were come to land, they saw a fire of coals there, and fish laid thereon, and bread. [10] Jesus saith unto them, Bring of the fish which ye have now caught. [11] Simon Peter went up, and drew the net to land full of great fishes, an hundred and fifty and three: and for all there were so many, yet was not the net broken. [12] Jesus saith unto them, Come and dine. And none of the disciples durst ask him, Who art thou? knowing that it was the Lord.*

That was quite a feast of God-made bread and roasted fish. More than anything this was a moment to feel at rest with Him again. It was here that Jesus restored Peter who had denied knowing Him. He asked him three times, "Do you love me," and each time Peter's yes removed a time when he had said, "I do not know Him." Unburdened of his guilt and the consciousness of sin—his denial, Peter would again be free to serve. Instead of follow me, this time, the Lord said feed my sheep.

Peter was again a fisher of men. His first catch was a real net breaker of 3000 souls. I remember watching a video at church. There were some men and children in the boat who were out on a lake to catch fish. They didn't even get a line in the water before the fish started jumping into the boat. There were so many fish leaping above the water that they were literally filling up the boat. I think that is how it felt to Peter that day he caught those 3000 souls. I fully expect an end time revival with a great haul of souls like that too. As Christians we are all fishing with Jesus.

Rev. Kathryn L. Smith

Acts 26:8 (KJV) *⁸ Why should it be thought a thing incredible with you, that God should raise the dead?*

Starting at Dead

The most final answer in the story of life was always death. Sickness might be temporary, but death was the end. "Once dead, only God can bring a person back to life. In the realm of the physical, He does that in the resurrection; and spiritually, He accomplishes it in the miracle of the new birth." (Smith p. 31) Only God could restore what was lost. God sometimes restored physical life where death had reigned. There were only a few recorded cases throughout history when someone was raised from the dead.

God began revealing that there was eternal life and a potential for resurrection early into the Old Testament. **Isaiah 25:8 (KJV)** *[8] He will swallow up death in victory; and the Lord GOD will wipe away tears from off all faces; and the rebuke of his people shall he take away from off all the earth: for the LORD hath spoken it.*

The power of God fell upon the Old Testament prophets and there are cases recorded of them raising the dead. One of them is the resureection of the son of a gentile woman. In order to bring life back into the dead it takes at least three of the gifts of the Spirit. To raise the dead boy meant that the prophet asked for a suspension of the laws of nature. That is the gift of miracles. For the mother or the prophet to ask for this took a gift of faith. The third gift was that of healing, in order for the boy to live they had to remove the sickness that had caused his death.

II Kings 4:18-35 (KJV) *[18] And when the child was grown, it fell on a day, that he went out to his father to the reapers. [19] And he said unto his father, My head, my head. And he said to a lad, Carry him to his mother. [20] And when he had taken him, and brought him to his mother, he sat on her knees till noon, and then died.* This woman had the faith to go to the prophet Elisha and expect him to restore life to her son. *[30] And the mother of the child said, As the LORD liveth, and as thy soul liveth, I will not leave thee. And he arose, and followed her... [32] And when Elisha was come into the house, behold, the child was dead, and laid upon his bed. [33] He went in therefore, and shut the door upon them twain, and prayed unto the LORD. [34] And he went up, and lay upon the child, and put his mouth upon his mouth, and his eyes upon his eyes, and his hands upon his hands: and he stretched himself* *upon the child; and the flesh of the child waxed warm. [35] Then he returned, and walked in the house to and fro; and went up, and stretched himself upon him: and the child sneezed seven times, and the child opened his eyes.* That is a miracle. The boy's body had grown cold. He did not respond the first time the prophet prayed. That man of God stayed in faith until life returned to that child.

There was a young woman that went to church with me over 30 years ago. She could not conceive and was very distraught. Our pastor at the time prayed that God would heal her and shortly after that she became pregnant. Nine months later she gave birth to a baby boy. When he was still a toddler he was taken to the hospital and our pastor was called. The doctors worked on him, but they could not get him breathing and they pronounced him dead. Our pastor took the child into his arms and prayed, and that boy took a deep breath. The doctors sent them home. Those doctors called it a miracle, they said we did nothing that helped him; it was all God.

Have you ever read about the anointing that lingered in the bones of the prophet Elisha? **II Kings 13:20-21 (KJV)** [20] *And Elisha died, and they buried him. And the bands of the Moabites invaded the land at the coming in of the year.* [21] *And it came to pass, as they were burying a man, that, behold, they spied a band of men; and they cast the man* *into the sepulchre of Elisha: and when the man was let down, and touched the bones of Elisha, he revived, and stood up on his feet.* There was so much of God in the man that even his dead dry bones possessed a powerful anointing. If a dead prophet under the Old Covenant had that kind of power residing in his bones, just imagine the power in the living believer.

Before we move on to the New Testament, I would like to look at an amazing image from the book of Ezekiel. **Ezekiel 37:1-13 (KJV)** *[1] The hand of the LORD was upon me, and carried me out in the spirit of the LORD, and set me down in the midst of the valley which was full of bones,* If it is the valley of dry bones it is because all of the fallen have been dead for a long time *[2] And caused me to pass by them round about: and, behold, there were very many in the open valley; and, lo, they were very dry.* The prophet was walking around in the middle of that valley. It was a graveyard. More accurately, it was probably a battlefield. Some place where they had fought and died and not even been buried. Long dead, these bones were all that was left of what had been real lives. It was impossible to tell which bones belonged to a single skeleton. There had been animal predators and weather to cause the full decay and scattering of what had been human bodies. They were almost but not quite forgotten. *[3] And he said unto me, Son* *of man, can these bones live? And I answered, O Lord GOD, thou knowest.* The prophet said that only God could know what potential there is in something so dead. But we also read in verse 1 that God's hand was upon Ezekiel. Ezekiel is no one without God—a zero if you like. It was not his ability, his past experiences; it was the Lord directing and touching and carrying Ezekiel that brought him to this dead place. Is there any hope for these?

Can life come where death has reigned? It was a question that we may have asked at one time or another about a part of our life, or a part of our ministry. It might be a question about someone we had seen fall to the ground wounded and damaged and who appeared to have let the life of God bleed out of them. Only where death has reigned can there be a resurrection. God wanted the prophet to see beyond the obvious, beyond the natural, into the place where faith connected with the Author of life itself.

Ezekiel 37:4-8 (KJV) *[4] Again he said unto me, Prophesy upon these bones, and say unto them, O ye dry bones, hear the word of the LORD. [5] Thus saith the Lord GOD unto these bones; Behold, I will cause breath to enter into you, and ye shall live:* He said I brought you here and I commanded you to walk where the dead are, and now I am asking you to speak life to them. It was a tall order. It took stepping out beyond the normal area of faith. It was asking for more than one miracle. There was no muscle or tissue left. The Amplified Bible says, *"I will lay sinews upon you, and will bring up flesh upon you and cover you with skin, and put breath and spirit in you, and you [dry bones] shall live; and you shall know, understand and realize, that I am the Lord [the Sovereign Ruler, calling forth loyalty and obedient service.]"* They were so dead it was just bones, just a remnant of what had been. It took a creative miracle just to begin. Ezekiel had nothing to work with except the Word of the Lord and that was more than enough. *[7] So I prophesied as I was commanded: and as I prophesied, there was a noise, and behold a shaking, and the bones came together, bone to his bone. [8] And when I beheld, lo, the sinews and the flesh came up upon them, and the skin covered them above: but there was no breath in them.*

The entire death and decay process was reversed. The bones reconnected, the rotten flesh and decay were gone, the bodies were restored; they looked good but they were still dead. No matter how good you look on the outside it is the spirit of God on the inside that brings life. You can dress up a dead body but it is still dead. I have only heard of one man with enough faith to walk into a funeral home and pull a body out of the casket and command it to live. That man was Smith Wigglesworth. He was a plumber turned evangelist in the early 1900's. He was documented to have raised five people from the dead, including one who had been embalmed, and laid out in his casket. That is powerful faith. It is God directed faith with God's own authority behind it. That does not happen by the will of man. The thing God was speaking to Ezekiel does not happen without the Lord either.

Ezekiel 37:9-10 (KJV) *[9] Then said he unto me, Prophesy unto the wind, prophesy, son of man, and say to the wind, Thus saith the Lord GOD; Come from the four winds, O breath, and breathe upon these slain, that they may live.* The Lord told Ezekiel to prophesy. He said speak to that dead bunch and command the wind to blow. He was told to speak for the breath of God to be restored in them. *[10] So I prophesied as he commanded me, and the breath came into them, and they lived, and stood up upon their feet, an exceeding great army.* I can imagine that killing field once soaked with their blood giving up its captives. I can see them standing there ready to fight again. Only God can do that.

Ezekiel 37:11-14 (KJV) *[11] Then he said unto me, Son of man, these bones are the whole house of Israel: behold, they say, Our bones are dried, and our hope is lost: we are cut off for our parts.* God was speaking to Israel and also in our time to believers. The whole of the church has been weary and broken and under siege. The bodies of believers were sick and damaged and the doctors gave their report that hope was gone, but God still has a say. *[12] Therefore prophesy and say unto them, Thus saith the Lord GOD; Behold, O my people, I will open your graves, and cause you to come up* *out of your graves, and bring you into the land of Israel. ^{13} And ye shall know that I am the LORD, when I have opened your graves, O my people, and brought you up out of your graves, ^{14} And shall put my spirit in you, and ye shall live, and I shall place you in your own land: then shall ye know that I the LORD have spoken it, and performed it, saith the LORD.* Come up out of the pit and out of that valley. Come up out of the graveyard. Let the dead things go, leave them behind.

God promised a 75 year old man that he would be a father. Abraham waited for the birth of his son for 25 years. He and Sarah were already well past the natural age of new parents. Sarah had been barren through decades. That appears to be a hopeless situation. Abraham looks at his destiny and says I am a zero. I am old and I have no son to leave my possessions or to carry on my linage. When all hope in the natural was lost, dead and buried, God renewed and revived it. God had taken him out and showed him the night sky and said that his descendants would be as numerous as those countless stars. [Gen 15:5] God had declared that it was through Isaac that the whole world would be blessed. Remember also that when asked to sacrifice his only son Isaac, the son of God's promise, Abraham obeyed. Knowing that all future generations were tied to that covenant promise, Abraham was willing to kill him. [Gen. 22:1-14] **Hebrews 11:17-19 (KJV)** *^{17} By faith Abraham,* *when he was tried, offered up Isaac: and he that had received the promises offered up his only begotten son,* [18] *Of whom it was said, That in Isaac shall thy seed be called:* [19] *Accounting that God was able to raise him up, even from the dead; from whence also he received him in a figure.* This clearly shows that he believed there was a potential for resurrection life. He could never have destroyed all of his future if he did not count God as powerful enough to resurrect his son and through him fulfill the promise of the Messiah.

David did not consider death to be the end either. He spoke of walking though death but not being held by it. **Psalm 23:1-6 (KJV)** [1] *The LORD is my shepherd; I shall not want.* [2] *He maketh me to lie down in green pastures: he leadeth me beside the still waters.* [3] *He restoreth my soul: he leadeth me in the paths of righteousness for his name's sake.* God is providing for me, I rest refreshed and I have all I need to eat and drink and He renews and restores my weary mind and the depths of my soul and spirit. He guides me day in and day out, and He orders my steps. I can walk as the righteous, because He has made me to be righteous. [4] *Yea, though I walk through the valley of the shadow of death, I will fear no evil: for thou art with me; thy rod and thy staff they comfort me.* Sometimes you have to go through the valley of the shadow of death so you can walk out on the other side. It is for the Father's glory. And it is only a shadow of death; real death has already been defeated. *⁵ Thou preparest a table before me in the presence of mine enemies:* Right there where the enemy thought I had lost all, right there where my broken and damaged body lay looking all dead and decayed, the Lord honored me, blessed me, fed me and made me His own. *thou anointest my head with oil; my cup runneth over.* To make the cup to run over was to invite the one it was poured out for, to stay forever. *⁶ Surely goodness and mercy shall follow me all the days of my life: and I will dwell in the house of the LORD forever.* Eternal life is the true victory over physical death.

There was always a promise of the Messiah. When Jesus came He freely raised the dead. **Luke 7:11-15 (KJV)** *¹¹ And it came to pass the day after, that he went into a city called Nain; and many of his disciples went with him, and much people. ¹² Now when he came nigh to the gate of the city, behold, there was a dead man carried out, the only son of his mother, and she was a widow: and much people of the city was with her. ¹³ And when the Lord saw her, he had compassion on her, and said unto her, Weep not. ¹⁴ And he came and touched the bier: and they that bare him stood still. And he said, Young man, I say unto thee, Arise. ¹⁵ And he that was dead* *sat up, and began to speak. And he delivered him to his mother.* That was not the only parent to receive their child alive after they had fallen victim to something that brought about their death.

Luke 8:41-42 (KJV) *[41] And, behold, there came a man named Jairus, and he was a ruler of the synagogue: and he fell down at Jesus' feet, and besought him that he would come into his house: [42] For he had one only daughter, about twelve years of age, and she lay a dying. But as he went the people thronged him.* Along the way there was a divine interruption. Jesus took time to heal the woman with an issue of blood. The Bible does not record Jairus urging Jesus to hurry or being frustrated by the delay. **Luke 8:40-56 (KJV)** *[49] While he yet spake, there cometh one from the ruler of the synagogue's house, saying to him, Thy daughter is dead; trouble not the Master. [50] But when Jesus heard it, he answered him, saying, Fear not: believe only, and she shall be made whole. [51] And when he came into the house, he suffered no man to go in, save Peter, and James, and John, and the father and the mother of the maiden. [52] And all wept, and bewailed her: but he said, Weep not; she is not dead, but sleepeth. [53] And they laughed him to scorn, knowing that she was dead. [54] And he put them all out, and took her by the hand, and called, saying, Maid, arise.* Jesus simply called to her like her parents did when they woke her from sleep. *[55] And her spirit came again, and she arose straightway: and he commanded to give her meat. [56] And her parents were astonished: but he charged* *them that they should tell no man what was done.* I wonder what became of that little girl who had once suffered in sickness and died, and was then snatched from the grip of death.

There is nothing more powerful than the Lord who created this entire universe. We are the people He placed here on earth. Once God pronounced life over us, death was defeated. He who is the resurrection and the life is still with us. Death is not an end any longer.

Starting With Zero

John 11:25-26 (KJV) *²⁵ Jesus said unto her, I am the resurrection, and the life: he that believeth in me, though he were dead, yet shall he live: ²⁶ And whosoever liveth and believeth in me shall never die.*

Lazarus Come Forth

Probably the best known case of raising the dead is that of Lazarus. The name Lazarus means God has helped. And we all know that he was most definitely helped. It was this undisputed miracle that caused great despair among the religious leaders in Jerusalem. **John 11:1 – 2 (KJV)** [1] *Now a certain man was sick, named Lazarus, of Bethany, the town of Mary and her sister Martha.* Bethany is about two miles outside of Jerusalem. Jesus had probably stayed in their home on His journey more than once. These three are mentioned in several places and so they were close friends.

Martha is the same one who wanted Jesus to order her sister to come help in the kitchen when Mary was kneeling at His feet listening to Him teach. Mary was almost always at His feet and for good reason. Most think she was delivered of many demons and had lived a very immoral life. Her heart was full of gratitude and hungry for both love and truth. *² (It was that Mary which anointed the Lord with ointment, and wiped his feet with her hair, whose brother Lazarus was sick.) ³ Therefore his sisters sent unto him, saying, Lord, behold, he whom thou lovest is sick.* When things got bad, they called on someone they knew could bring healing and deliverance and life. When you get in distress, call on Jesus. *⁴ When Jesus heard that, he said, This sickness is not unto death, but for the glory of God, that the Son of God might be glorified thereby.* NIV- *⁴When he heard this, Jesus said, "This sickness will not end in death.* Considering the situation, that was faith being spoken. Those around Him thought He said the sickness was nothing to worry about and Lazarus would not die. Jesus never said Lazarus would not die, just that in the end God would get glory and that there would be some kind of intervention.

Jesus indicated that though Lazarus would die, death was temporary. The attack upon Lazarus was for a purpose; it was to bring God glory so that God's Son might be glorified through it. *⁵ Now Jesus loved Martha, and her sister, and Lazarus. ⁶ When he had heard therefore that he was sick, he abode two days still in the same place where he was.* At this point He could have spoken the word and healed their brother. Jesus had spoken healing to others from a distance and they were made whole. He chose not to do so here, because they were preparing for a greater miracle.

Jesus was in Perea about thirty miles away, so the message that Lazarus was sick most likely took two or three days to arrive. If Jesus had started toward them the minute He heard of the need, Lazarus would have still died before He arrived. We know Jesus waited two more days, so now it has been four or five days since the sisters sent for Him. In the natural, Lazarus is dead. The Lord loved this family. He went at the time when God could get the most glory from His visit; when man could not assume the sickness had subsided on its own, and when the miracle of the resurrection was undeniable. Just because Jesus loves you does not mean He comes running the moment you need Him, or you cry out for help. Sometimes our best plan is not the best God has to offer. Maybe your good idea is not a God idea. It may seem like His delay means Jesus failed, or that He is late. Let me assure you, Jesus can't fail and He is never late.

John 11:7 - 16 (KJV) [7] *Then after that saith he to his disciples, Let us go into Judaea again.* [8] *His disciples say unto him, Master, the Jews of late sought to stone thee; and goest thou thither again?* They had reason to be concerned. The disciples knew there was danger and deep seated hostility toward Jesus and even His followers, so they did not take the thought lightly *⁹ Jesus answered, Are there not twelve hours in the day? If any man walk in the day, he stumbleth not, because he seeth the light of this world. ¹⁰ But if a man walk in the night, he stumbleth, because there is no light in him.*

He is talking in this whole chapter about the struggle between light and darkness, good and evil, life and death and ultimately between God and Satan. He is the one who said I am the light, and the life and He says if you really walk close to me, you won't fall. He was saying for the entire time that the Father had planned for Him to be here; for the entire time He had work to do, the world would not be able to stop His plan. They could not kill Jesus before the time, and He knew His time was not up. He would not be murdered. There would be a time to lay down His life when He would become the Father's sacrifice. *¹¹ These things said he: and after that he saith unto them, Our friend Lazarus sleepeth; but I go, that I may awake him out of sleep. ¹² Then said his disciples, Lord, if he sleep, he shall do well. ¹³ Howbeit Jesus spake of his death: but they thought that he had spoken of taking of rest in sleep.* They misunderstood the Master. *¹⁴ Then said Jesus unto them plainly, Lazarus is dead. ¹⁵ And I am glad for your sakes that I was not there, to the intent ye may believe; nevertheless let us go unto him.*

The raising of Lazarus from the dead was an essential display of His power, and the resurrection from the dead is a crucial belief of the Christian faith, not only could Jesus come back from the grave, He could give that life to men as well. The miracle of the resurrection was greater than the healing would have been. Sure, it would have been less painful for Mary and Martha and probably for Lazarus. It would have been easier for Jesus to speak the word of healing when He first heard of the need. But this was an essential event—it was proof that He had power over death. *[16] Then said Thomas, which is called Didymus, unto his fellow disciples, Let us also go, that we may die with him.* Good old Thomas, pessimistic to a fault, was always seeing the dark side of things; the negative, the danger or the sorrow. Thomas was proclaimed a doubter later on when he said I will not believe until I touch the nail prints in His hands, but here he is loyal. Even if it means we die, I will follow you and go to your friend.

John 11:17-27 (KJV) *[17] Then when Jesus came, he found that he had lain in the grave four days already.* The Jews believed that the spirit of a man stayed near the body for three days. The fact that Lazarus was dead for four days made the resurrection more dramatic and put their foolish ideas to rest. *[18] Now Bethany was nigh unto*

Jerusalem, about fifteen furlongs off: [19] *And many of the Jews came to Martha and Mary, to comfort them concerning their brother.* [20] *Then Martha, as soon as she heard that Jesus was coming, went and met him: but Mary sat still in the house.*

The exchange between Martha and Jesus could be called a lesson in faith. For faith to be effective, it must be current, alive, and complete. It must have the elements of trust, emotional response, belief and understanding and then it must be loyal enough to rely on the relationship with God to produce the best result. [21] *Then said Martha unto Jesus, Lord, if thou hadst been here, my brother had not died.* That sounds like regret, even a little like an accusation. [22] *But I know, that even now, whatsoever thou wilt ask of God, God will give it thee.* She was saying that her heart had confidence in Jesus as a friend and as God's representative; however, she was not saying you can raise him now, or the conversation that follows would have indicated that. [23] *Jesus saith unto her, Thy brother shall rise again.* [24] *Martha saith unto him, I know that he shall rise again in the resurrection at the last day.* Her comment was about like someone saying you will see them again, in heaven. It sounds good but it was not enough. The Jews saw a final end time resurrection as a future potential, but

Jesus was the present assurance of what they only hoped for.

In Hebrews we read, *"Faith is the substance of things hoped for the evidence of that yet unseen."* Jesus was trying to encourage her to look to what was beyond the death of her brother. He was still able to change the circumstances, and He wanted her to reach into the faith realm for more. Jesus was resurrection in reality, in the now, right there to meet her need and He was trying to encourage her to accept that. *^{25} Jesus said unto her, I am the resurrection, and the life:* There is another of those I am statements; I am the way, I am the truth, I am the light, I am the bread of life, I am the resurrection and the life. *he that believeth in me, though he were dead, yet shall he live: ^{26} And whosoever liveth and believeth in me shall never die. Believest thou this?* Whoever believes in Jesus Christ has spiritual life now and resurrection life now, and eternal life now. Death cannot conquer or diminish that life in any way. *^{27} She saith unto him, Yea, Lord: I believe that thou art the Christ, the Son of God, which should come into the world.* The resurrection is a personal communion with the Lord of life; it is an ongoing relationship with the Christ, not just something He gives us. The Lord endues us with His own presence. We are united with the One who is resurrection. She had to know who He was and then trust in that; Paul said it too in **II Timothy 1:12 (NIV)** *¹²That is why I am suffering as I am. Yet I am not ashamed, because I know whom I have believed, and am convinced that he is able to guard what I have entrusted to him for that day.*

The believer must not just know about faith, but remain vitally connected to the One in whom he believes. We trust the One we have walked with and talked with. People often make the mistake of having faith in their own faith, but we have to recognize that it is He who is faithful and our confidence is not in our prayer but the One we pray to. We must keep our eyes on Him alone.

John 11:28 - 37 (KJV) *²⁸ And when she had so said, she went her way, and called Mary her sister secretly, saying, The Master is come, and calleth for thee.* A better translation is the Master is here and seeks you. That is the best reason to respond; He is Lord and He calls you to Him. He is Master over life and death, Master in her darkest hour, Master and therefore the One to obey. *²⁹ As soon as she heard that, she arose quickly, and came unto him. ³⁰ Now Jesus was not yet come into the town, but was in that place where Martha met him. ³¹ The Jews then which were with her in the house, and comforted her, when they saw Mary, that she rose up hastily and went out, followed her, saying,*

She goeth unto the grave to weep there. ³² Then when Mary was come where Jesus was, and saw him, she fell down at his feet, saying unto him, Lord, if thou hadst been here, my brother had not died. She spoke the same words as her sister. I think they are words the women had shared in private. Mary fell at His feet; just like when she sat there and listened to His words, just like when she knelt there to wash His feet with her tears. Her normal posture was one of worship. ³³ *When Jesus therefore saw her weeping, and the Jews also weeping which came with her, he groaned in the spirit, and was troubled,* He spoke no words, but He groaned in His spirit. Sometimes there are just no words to say, and nothing to pray. In those times, a moan or a groan, a sigh or our tears speak something our Father understands. ³⁴ *And said, Where have ye laid him? They said unto him, Lord, come and see. ³⁵ Jesus wept.*

Some say Jesus wept out of compassion for this sister; some say He was sorrowing over their lack of faith. Some even think this refers to the weight of mankind's fallen nature that brought about death, and the sin payment that He bore within His heart until He could grasp it on the cross. Regardless it probably also included a sense of indignation and sorrow for the hypocrisy that they evidently held as mourners who would later accuse and doubt and persecute the Lord. Regardless, He shed tears. He felt like us, hurt like us. Jesus understood the frailty of man and the pressures of sin and death. He saw how mankind deemed death to be final, but He was about to shake up their theology.

John 11:36-37 *^{36} Then said the Jews, Behold how he loved him! ^{37} And some of them said, Could not this man, which opened the eyes of the blind, have caused that even this man should not have died?* Have you ever known people that no matter what anyone does for them, or even what God does it is just never enough? They only knew His works, because they did not seem to know Him personally, and they did not honor Him with their words. If they only knew His heart, they would not condemn Him.

John 11:38 - 44 (KJV) *^{38} Jesus therefore again groaning in himself cometh to the grave. It was a cave, and a stone lay upon it. ^{39} Jesus said, Take ye away the stone. Martha, the sister of him that was dead, saith unto him, Lord, by this time he stinketh: for he hath been dead four days.* He needed the one in charge to grow enough in faith to order it done, so he challenged Martha's faith, and looked to her for a response. NIV *"But, Lord," said Martha, the sister of the dead man, "by this time there is a bad odor, for he has been there four* *days."* The reason they put all the flowers and ointments on the body was that no one wanted to remember the decaying smell of their loved one. After four days in a warm climate without embalming fluid, she was right—decay would have set in. But Jesus wanted her out of her natural fleshly mind and into an area of confidence in Him. *[40] Jesus saith unto her, Said I not unto thee, that, if thou wouldest believe, thou shouldest see the glory of God?* We do not hear her approve the opening of the grave, but we know she did. *[41] Then they took away the stone from the place where the dead was laid.* He asked her to look at the facts and then weigh them against the One who did the impossible. She spoke the facts, but He who is the truth spoke what was higher than the facts. Truth always triumphs over facts. Her faith was willing to suffer shame and embarrassment rather than deny the Lord's request. *And Jesus lifted up his eyes, and said, Father, I thank thee that thou hast heard me. [42] And I knew that thou hearest me always: but because of the people which stand by I said it, that they may believe that thou hast sent me.*

Jesus lived a life of perfect obedience, perfect communion with the Father; He knew God heard Him and responded. When did God hear Him? He heard Jesus say, *"This sickness will not end in death."* God also heard Him say, *"I go to wake him."* God heard Jesus tell Martha, *"I am the resurrection and the life. Your brother will live again."* Every time death came to the door, Jesus answered with faith and each of those times His words of life were sown into the atmosphere. Jesus had been preparing for this moment with every word He spoke. Jesus wanted all the people gathered there to know it was God who gave life to Lazarus. *[43] And when he thus had spoken, he cried with a loud voice, Lazarus, come forth. [44] And he that was dead came forth, bound hand and foot with graveclothes: and his face was bound about with a napkin. Jesus saith unto them, Loose him, and let him go.*

Some people think that if Jesus had not used his name, when He called to Lazarus that every man in those graves would have come out. Not even the grave has the power to hold you back when Jesus calls. He came out wrapped like a mummy. Jesus had done what they could not, so He had them do what they could which was to manually pull away the grave clothes. Lazarus was no longer bound by death so the trappings of death should not be on him. The trappings of death have no place on the man who is redeemed; that is you. You are free from the finality and stench and judgment that are attached to death; walk free.

There should have been great joy. That joy was mixed with fear. The Jews feared that they would lose the little authority they had left to sway the people. They recognized a power greater than their own but some of them did not honor God or desire more.

John 11:45 (NIV) *[45]Therefore many of the Jews who had come to visit Mary, and had seen what Jesus did, put their faith in him.* Lazarus was a living testament to the power of God that abode in Jesus. In order for Lazarus to return to the living, Jesus had to restore life, heal the sickness that had caused his death, and reverse the decaying process. **John 12:9-11 (KJV)** *[9] Much people of the Jews therefore knew that he was there: and they came not for Jesus' sake only, but that they might see Lazarus also, whom he had raised from the dead. [10] But the chief priests consulted that they might put Lazarus also to death; [11] Because that by reason of him many of the Jews went away, and believed on Jesus.*

The crowds that came threw wood on the fires of fear and indignation. The flames of jealousy and hatred burned hot against Jesus, until they determined to kill Him. **John 11:45 - 57 (NIV)** *[46]But some of them went to the Pharisees and told them what Jesus had done. [47]Then the chief priests and the Pharisees called a meeting of the Sanhedrin. "What are we accomplishing?" they asked. "Here is this man performing many miraculous signs.* They could not question His works, but they were willing to put aside the miraculous to keep what they saw as their advantage. ⁴⁸*If we let him go on like this, everyone will believe in him, and then the Romans will come and take away both our place and our nation."* ⁴⁹*Then one of them, named Caiaphas, who was high priest that year, spoke up, "You know nothing at all!* ⁵⁰*You do not realize that it is better for you that one man die for the people than that the whole nation perish."*

This was the final straw; the religious elite could take no more. As High Priest, Caiaphas spoke prophetically that Jesus would die for the Jews that had Him arrested and for the gentiles that carried out His sentence. The blood shed would be for all mankind and salvation would open what would be the tombs of millions of future believers. From that moment on, the cross was always in the foreground.

One reason the Romans were so afraid of Jesus was that He could maintain an army miraculously. He could heal anyone sick or wounded. Jesus could also raise the dead. More than once He fed a multitude with just a tiny provision. There was no way to defeat any army He gathered. Even when they nailed Jesus to a cross it was not the end of Him. Jesus came back to life victorious over death; there was no power that could stop Him. He who is resurrection life, can and will change what has been dead. We are marked for resurrection because we have been born of His Spirit. His life is in us now. We have eternal life, real life, flowing through our veins. Since nothing could stop Him, nothing should stop us.

If it was Lazarus who lay in the grave or the widow's son on his way to be buried or Jairus' daughter being resurrected, it is because recently there was a death and a loss. Loss and death will try to take us to a place of no return, but death is not the final word for the believer.

Jesus freely showed that death was never the will of the Father. He did not only deal with physical death, but with the root cause and gave unto His followers the promise of eternal life. **John 6:38-44 (KJV)** *38 For I came down from heaven, not to do mine own will, but the will of him that sent me. 39 And this is the Father's will which hath sent me, that of all which he hath given me I should lose nothing, but should raise it up again at the last day. 40 And this is the will of him that sent me, that every one which seeth the Son, and believeth on him, may have everlasting life: and I will raise him up at the last day. 41 The Jews then murmured at him, because he said, I am the bread which came down from heaven. 42 And they said, Is not this Jesus, the son of Joseph, whose father and mother we know? how is it then that he saith, I came down from heaven? 43 Jesus therefore answered and said unto them, Murmur not among yourselves. 44 No man can* *come to me, except the Father which hath sent me draw him: and I will raise him up at the last day.*

God did more in Jesus and His resurrection than was ever done in any man. "Enoch and Elijah had cheated death, and numerous others had been resuscitated from the dead to die again later. But Jesus had freely enter into death, destroyed it, and risen out of it never to die again. In His resurrection, the reign of death was declared over and finished and every man and woman carried in Him out of its grasp." (Smith p. 88)

Ephesians 2:4-10 (KJV) *[4] But God, who is rich in mercy, for his great love wherewith he loved us, [5] Even when we were dead in sins, hath quickened us together with Christ, (by grace ye are saved;) [6] And hath raised us up together, and made us sit together in heavenly places in Christ Jesus: [7] That in the ages to come he might shew the exceeding riches of his grace in his kindness toward us through Christ Jesus. [8] For by grace are ye saved through faith; and that not of yourselves: it is the gift of God: [9] Not of works, lest any man should boast. [10] For we are his workmanship, created in Christ Jesus unto good works, which God hath before ordained that we should walk in them.*

"Faith is a response to knowing what God says He will do for you." (Prince 4/20/18) The Lord Jesus is alive from the dead and those of us who really know that we are saved are living in

Him. Our life in Christ might begin on earth but it will take us to His home in heaven. Death will never destroy us, only promote us.

I Corinthians 2:7-10 (KJV) *⁷ But we speak the wisdom of God in a mystery, even the hidden wisdom, which God ordained before the world unto our glory: ⁸ Which none of the princes of this world knew: for had they known it, they would not have crucified the Lord of glory.* The devil didn't know that bringing Jesus to death would defeat death. He didn't know that resurrection life would not just restore the Messiah, but would restore every man who would ever believe in Him. *⁹ But as it is written, Eye hath not seen, nor ear heard, neither have entered into the heart of man, the things which God hath prepared for them that love him. ¹⁰ But God hath revealed them unto us by his Spirit: for the Spirit searcheth all things, yea, the deep things of God.*

The power of the cross is not just that sin is gone and judgement will not fall upon you. It is that you can walk free in life. The power of the cross is that real life is yours—that His resurrection life is in you now. You have life inside.

Speaking to what is dead and dry to come alive has no potential of victory unless it is God who speaks. If God is speaking, nothing dead stays dead. If it is God speaking, then there isn't anything or anyone who can resist His words. He can make you alive again. There was a death sentence on each of us; there was no chance, no hope. He who is the resurrection and the life has freely given us that life.

I Corinthians 15:54-55 (NIV) *[54] When the perishable has been clothed with the imperishable, and the mortal with immortality, then the saying that is written will come true: "Death has been swallowed up in victory." [55] "Where, O death, is your victory? Where, O death, is your sting?"* The Message Bible says, "Death who is afraid of you now?" It was the One with resurrection life that spoke to death as if it was nothing.

There is coming a day when the slain of the battlefield and those buried in the grave will hear the Lord call. It will be greater than what happened in Ezekiel's day. In that day, bone and flesh that have been long dead will come together and form new resurrected bodies. **I Corinthians 6:14 (KJV)** *[14] And God hath both raised up the Lord, and will also raise up us by his own power.*

I Thessalonians 4:13-17 (KJV) *[13] But I would not have you to be ignorant, brethren, concerning them which are asleep, that ye sorrow not, even as others which have no hope. [14] For if we believe that Jesus died and rose again, even so them* *also which sleep in Jesus will God bring with him.* *[15] For this we say unto you by the word of the Lord, that we which are alive and remain unto the coming of the Lord shall not prevent them which are asleep. [16] For the Lord himself shall descend from heaven with a shout, with the voice of the archangel, and with the trump of God: and the dead in Christ shall rise first: [17] Then we which are alive and remain shall be caught up together with them in the clouds, to meet the Lord in the air: and so shall we ever be with the Lord.* Every vaporized body from the World Trade Centers will come together. Every bit of bone and flesh that ever lived will hear the voice of the Lord calling life into them. Every sailor buried at sea will come up out of that ocean; my dad will rise up out of the cemetery. No part of death will be able to hold them back. They are already marked for resurrection.

You are marked for resurrection. You are the born-again. As the resurrected while still living, there is nothing damaged that can't be made whole. Where there was lack there can be provision. You are not finished. If your life was a book or a movie no one has written "THE END." While we are on this earth we are here to be a resurrected army ready to fight again, able to withstand any assault. We were nothing, our value no more than those who lie in the grave, but God took our emptiness and now we are empowered by the Spirit of the Living God. Death has no right to us, no power over us. There is resurrection life in us.

Get up out of that dead place. Throw off the smelly rags that stink of death; you are alive. You get up and nothing dead comes with you. The same Lord who saved you is still speaking life to the dead. There is resurrection life in you. Jesus, who is life, poured out His life on the cross. Start at zero, at death because then you can see His provision then it is possible to realize that it has all been Him. He died so you could live victorious. You have resureection life in you.

Starting With Zero

Psalm 37:25 (KJV) *²⁵ I have been young, and now am old; yet have I not seen the righteous forsaken, nor his seed begging bread.*

Supernatural Supply

God created Adam and Eve so that He could pour out love to them. God was always a giver; He wanted to give the best to His children. It was not until the fall that mankind had any needs that were not already supplied in abundance.

We have already looked at the widow's oil that flowed until there was no pot left to put any more oil in. Similarly, we discussed the widow from Zarephath who fed the prophet Elijah, herself, and her son for over three years on a supply so small it was not even a good meal for one person. "God has not changed. He has more to give than we'll ever have the capacity to receive. And, amazingly, as we humbly receive, we are transformed into givers." (Fry p. 65) That widow's miracle was dependent upon obedience. Elisha had her sow what she had so she could receive a harvest. She and her son were at the point of starvation. The prophet says do as you planned but first give me a little bit of bread and some water.

We also know that God rained down food in the desert for the entire nation of Israel every day while they traveled through the wilderness. Just for fun I did the math, 365 days a year, two meals per person for 40 years, which is 29,200 meals for each person who wandered in the wilderness. That is millions of meals. David said, "**Psalm 37:25 (KJV)** *[25] I have been young, and now am old; yet have I not seen the righteous forsaken, nor his seed begging bread.*" God never disappointed them, never forgot them and never forsook them. We have a new a better covenant and His promises are more sure now than they have ever been. How is it that we worry that we will not have enough?

Matthew 6:25-33 (KJV) *[25] Therefore I say unto you, Take no thought for your life, what ye shall eat, or what ye shall drink; nor yet for your body, what ye shall put on. Is not the life more than meat, and the body than raiment? [26] Behold the fowls of the air: for they sow not, neither do they reap, nor gather into barns; yet your heavenly Father feedeth them. Are ye not much better than they? [27] Which of you by taking thought can add one cubit unto his stature? [28] And why take ye thought for raiment? Consider the lilies of the field, how they grow; they toil not, neither do they spin: [29] And yet I say unto you, That even Solomon in all his glory was not arrayed like one of these. [30] Wherefore, if God so clothe the grass of the field, which today is, and tomorrow is cast into the oven, shall he not much more clothe you, O ye of little* faith? *³¹ Therefore take no thought, saying, What shall we eat? or, What shall we drink? or, Wherewithal shall we be clothed? ³² (For after all these things do the Gentiles seek:) for your heavenly Father knoweth that ye have need of all these things. ³³ But seek ye first the kingdom of God, and his righteousness; and all these things shall be added unto you.*

Practically speaking, all of us want to be sure we have proper resources for our families. God has already promised us provision and we have seen Him do the miraculous when necessary to meet the natural needs of His people. God never intended for us to have just enough. He planned for us to be prosperous. "True prosperity is the ability to use God's power to meet the needs of mankind in any realm of life." (Copeland p. 26) Real prosperity is having enough to meet all my own needs and to minister freely to others.

Mark 6:33-44 (KJV) *³³ And the people saw them departing, and many knew him, and ran afoot thither out of all cities, and outwent them, and came together unto him. ³⁴ And Jesus, when he came out, saw much people, and was moved with compassion toward them, because they were as sheep not having a shepherd: and he began to teach them many things. ³⁵ And when the day was now far spent, his disciples came unto him, and said, This is a desert place, and now the time is far passed: ³⁶ Send them away, that they may go into the country* *round about, and into the villages, and buy themselves bread: for they have nothing to eat.* ³⁷ *He answered and said unto them, Give ye them to eat. And they say unto him, Shall we go and buy two hundred pennyworth of bread, and give them to eat?* They said if we paid a full year's wages, we could not even give each man a small bite of food. They were looking in the natural, but the Creator of all that ever was, stood there ready to make provision. I like the way John tells the story.

John 6:5-14 (KJV) ⁵ *When Jesus then lifted up his eyes, and saw a great company come unto him, he saith unto Philip, Whence shall we buy bread, that these may eat?* ⁶ *And this he said to prove him: for he himself knew what he would do.* ⁷ *Philip answered him, Two hundred pennyworth of bread is not sufficient for them, that every one of them may take a little.* ⁸ *One of his disciples, Andrew, Simon Peter's brother, saith unto him,* ⁹ *There is a lad here, which hath five barley loaves, and two small fishes: but what are they among so many?* ¹⁰ *And Jesus said, Make the men sit down. Now there was much grass in the place. So the men sat down, in number about five thousand.* ¹¹ *And Jesus took the loaves; and when he had given thanks, he distributed to the disciples, and the disciples to them that were set down; and likewise of the fishes as much as they would.* ¹² *When they* *were filled, he said unto his disciples, Gather up the fragments that remain, that nothing be lost.* [13] *Therefore they gathered them together, and filled twelve baskets with the fragments of the five barley loaves, which remained over and above unto them that had eaten.* [14] *Then those men, when they had seen the miracle that Jesus did, said, This is of a truth that prophet that should come into the world.*

Jesus took what they did have, just a small boy's lunch, and blessed it. He got it into His hands. He broke it and distributed it. Each of the disciples held a bit of fish and bread and as they gave it out, it multiplied. One evangelist said every broken piece became a whole one. The disciples then broke them and again they held two whole rolls. While I don't know how the multiplication came, I do know that it was more than enough. If every man there had a very small family of just a wife and two children, which was quite rare in those days, it would mean that five small rolls and a couple of fish filets filled up over 20,000 people. I know for me the miracle would have been worth noting if only fifty were filled, but we have a God of more than enough. Jesus said gather up what is leftover so nothing is wasted. They gathered more than they started with. I like to think that a little boy went home with a great story to tell his family. He says something like, "Mommy look at all the bread and fish I brought home. I gave my lunch to Jesus and everyone ate and He sent home all these baskets full of food to say thank you." I can't really imagine that family worrying about provision again.

Jesus fed the multitudes twice. First, He provided for the 5000 and then a group of 4000. **Mark 8:1-9 (KJV)** *[1] In those days the multitude being very great, and having nothing to eat, Jesus called his disciples unto him, and saith unto them, [2] I have compassion on the multitude, because they have now been with me three days, and have nothing to eat: [3] And if I send them away fasting to their own houses, they will faint by the way: for divers of them came from far. [4] And his disciples answered him, From whence can a man satisfy these men with bread here in the wilderness? [5] And he asked them, How many loaves have ye? And they said, Seven. [6] And he commanded the people to sit down on the ground: and he took the seven loaves, and gave thanks, and brake, and gave to his disciples to set before them; and they did set them before the people. [7] And they had a few small fishes: and he blessed, and commanded to set them also before them. [8] So they did eat, and were filled: and they took up of the broken meat that was left seven baskets. [9] And they that had eaten were about four thousand: and he sent them away.* If I read that right, Jesus did more with less. He can always do more with less. If I decrease He can increase and it will get done because He is enough.

Kenneth Copeland teaches that God prospers us through an extended hand. "God has a highly organized system to meet the needs of every facet of your life. The World's system of meeting our needs works exactly opposite from God's system. God's system is totally adequate." (Copeland p. 21) The world says if you only have a little hold on to it tightly, but God loves those who receive His blessings with an open hand, ready to share with others. That is what the boy with the loaves and fishes did. It is what the woman with the tiny bit of meal and oil did. They shared freely out of their own need and made way for supernatural supply.

In his book, *I Am, the Unveiling of God*, Steve Fry shares a dream with his readers. In the dream, a man went to both heaven and hell. First, he entered into a banquet room filled with wonderful food but each person around the table looked emaciated and desperate. There was a stench of rotting flesh. Each man had bound to his hand a long fork measuring over two foot in length. When they tried to eat they could not get the food into their mouths. Next the man entered what he thought was heaven. The same beautiful banquet table filled to overflowing with food. The people here had the same forks bound to their hands, but they were not angry or fearful or starving. Instead each gently and lovingly used his utensil to feed another. (Fry p. 62-64) If we are less concerned with ourselves we will not only have life for an eternity, but we will have a blessed life that starts our eternity right where we are. Those who are ready to share what they have will always have enough. Since the Word of God shows us that God can provide a table in the wilderness to feed the hungry, we have to act as if it is still true.

Martha should have known that she didn't have to work so hard. Yes, Jesus traveled with a large group of followers. Of course, any hostess would want to feed such a special guest well, but she could have relaxed and enjoyed the Lord's visit. **Luke 10:38-42 (KJV)** *[38] Now it came to pass, as they went, that he entered into a certain village: and a certain woman named Martha received him into her house. [39] And she had a sister called Mary, which also sat at Jesus' feet, and heard his word. [40] But Martha was cumbered about much serving,* I understand that she wanted everything to be perfect for her guests. I feel that way too and I am not entertaining the Lord and the crowd that followed Him. She busied herself in the kitchen and then she got frustrated. *[40] But Martha was cumbered about much serving, and came to him, and said, Lord, dost thou not care that my sister hath left me to serve alone? bid her therefore that she help me. [41] And Jesus answered and said unto her, Martha, Martha, thou art careful and troubled about many things: [42] But one thing is needful: and Mary hath chosen that good part, which shall not be taken away from her.* Martha could have walked out of that hot kitchen and sat down with Mary at the Master's feet and said I know you can multiply the bread and stew I made earlier for your disciples and I just want to be near you. Don't you think Jesus would have been pleased to hear her say that?

Jesus actually rebuked His followers one time when they worried about food to the point that they missed His message. **Matthew 16:8-12 (KJV)** *⁸ Which when Jesus perceived, he said unto them, O ye of little faith, why reason ye among yourselves, because ye have brought no bread? ⁹ Do ye not yet understand, neither remember the five loaves of the five thousand, and how many baskets ye took up? ¹⁰ Neither the seven loaves of the four thousand, and how many baskets ye took up? ¹¹ How is it that ye do not understand that I spake it not to you concerning bread, that ye should beware of the leaven of the Pharisees and of the Sadducees? ¹² Then understood they how that he bade them not beware of the leaven of bread, but of the doctrine of the Pharisees and of the Sadducees.* Jesus could provide a meal any time it was needed and He wanted them to take the care of provision off their radar and think spiritually.

God still wants us to trust in Him for our needs, and He provides for us as we trust Him. In the 1980's Jeanie, dear friend, stopped by my home unexpectedly. She told me that she was trying to get to town and she had a bad tire. Both of our husbands were at work. We could hear the air escaping from the tire, and it was already nearly flat. We prayed that God would keep enough air in it to get to a garage without damaging the tire or the rim. The closest place we knew was about seven miles away. I drove behind her so she would have a ride home, and we both prayed the whole way. When we arrived at the garage, her tire had more air in it than when we left my driveway. Only God could have done that. We were desperate—we had a need and we knew that God always responded to faith. We asked for and received a supernatural supply of air. Her tire was not damaged further and once they removed the screw she had driven over, the repair was only $5. God will do whatever His children need if they will ask in faith.

God has revealed His nature as the El Shaddai. He is the One with abundant supply. "He IS the All-Sufficient One. He is not just the God of yesterday; He's the God of NOW. He didn't say, "I'm the God who WAS more than enough." NO! He didn't say, "I'm the God who WILL BE more than enough." He said, I AM El Shaddai." (Hagin p. 6) He is the One who continually pours out heaps of blessing and a great provision. He will sustain you; you can never run Him dry.

My mother once told me about an elderly woman who lived in the country back in the 1940's. She lived all alone, and one year during a drought the old woman fell and broke her leg badly. Because she lived so far out in the woods, no one knew she was injured. She could not go for help, there was no phone so she set her leg the best she could and drug herself around the cabin until help came. Normally, the woman would have gone to a nearby stream every morning for water but it was too far to reach in her condition. The first day she pulled herself out to the rain barrel on the porch and she could see about an inch of water in the barrel. She looked to heaven and said, "This is all I have but I know you have all I need." She drew water from that barrel for six weeks. It was her only source of water for cooking and drinking and bathing. It never did rain, but the barrel did not go dry until the woman was able to walk down to the stream. That sounds like supernatural supply to me.

II Corinthians 9:8-11 (AMP) *8 And God is able to make all grace (every favor and earthly blessing) come to you in abundance, so that you may always and under all circumstances and whatever the need, be self-sufficient—possessing enough to require no aid or support and furnished in abundance for every good work and charitable donation...10 And [God] Who provides seed for the sower and bread for eating will also provide and multiply your [resources for] sowing, and increase the fruits of your righteousness [which manifests itself in active goodness, kindness and charity,] 11 Thus you will be enriched in all things and in every way, so that you can be generous...*

The Lord wants us blessed so that we can be a blessing. Our church runs a food pantry and we are honored to help feed the hungry in our community. Actually, most weeks we provide food for as many families outside the church as there are members inside the church. Whenever our shelves get low, a supply comes in. God has always provided for us. As His children, we need to expect not only enough for ourselves, but an overflow to share with others. He is the God of supernatural supply. His love compels Him to meet the needs of His children. We can trust the One who fed the multitudes and provided water for the thirsty. With God we will always have more than enough.

Starting With Zero

Rev. Kathryn L. Smith

Exodus 14:13 (KJV) *[13] And Moses said unto the people, Fear ye not, stand still, and see the salvation of the LORD...*

Surrounded

Generally speaking, we do not like to feel trapped or surrounded. We want to know we have a way of escape. We are no different from the people who lived in the days of Moses. His job was to lead a multitude to the Promised Land, but before they had even made it out of Egypt they were standing with their backs against the wall.

Exodus 14:10-16 (KJV) *^{10} And when Pharaoh drew nigh, the children of Israel lifted up their eyes, and, behold, the Egyptians marched after them; and they were sore afraid: and the children of Israel cried out unto the LORD. ^{11} And they said unto Moses, Because there were no graves in Egypt, hast thou taken us away to die in the wilderness? wherefore hast thou dealt thus with us, to carry us forth out of Egypt? ^{12} Is not this the word that we did tell thee in Egypt, saying, Let us alone, that we may serve the Egyptians? For it had been better for us to serve the Egyptians, than that we should die in the wilderness.* Welcome to the joy of leadership. The first problem that comes along and the masses respond in fear and blame their leader. *^{13} And Moses said unto the people, Fear ye not, stand still,* *and see the salvation of the LORD, which he will shew to you today: for the Egyptians whom ye have seen today, ye shall see them again no more forever.* Those are big promises considering the situation. The most powerful army on earth is chasing this untrained and mostly unarmed group of ex-slaves. There is nowhere to run. They are trapped between the raging hordes of chariots and soldiers and water. They can't get across the sea in the natural. They have every right to see disaster about to strike if they forget that the Most High is with them. *[14] The LORD shall fight for you, and ye shall hold your peace. [15] And the LORD said unto Moses, Wherefore criest thou unto me? speak unto the children of Israel, that they go forward: [16] But lift thou up thy rod, and stretch out thine hand over the sea, and divide it: and the children of Israel shall go on dry ground through the midst of the sea.* God said, just keep marching right across that barrier. "To human logic and feelings, the word of God made no sense. To go forward was to walk into the Red Sea! What could the lifting of a rod do to open a way through the sea? Nothing made sense—obedience to God was to go against all common sense, logic and feelings. Moses acted out of sheer will, acting as if God's word was true even though he could not understand." (Smith p. 228) So if you are at the sea, keep walking. He will open up the sea so you can walk right through it. They did turn away from looking at their enemies and trust at least a little in the God of Israel and sure enough they got through on dry ground.

"When the children of Israel arrived safely on the other side, the women got out their musical instruments and began to sing and dance. In the song the Spirit of God gave them it said, **Exodus 15:8 (KJV)** [8] *And with the blast of thy nostrils the waters were gathered together, the floods stood upright as an heap, and the depths were congealed in the heart of the sea.* 'Congealed' water is frozen water. God made the water stand up on both sides like a wall." (Hagin p. 3) I am not sure if it was cold and frozen like ice, or just hardened and held back. What I do know is that they walked through on dry ground and when their enemies tried it, God withdrew His hand and they drowned in the same sea.

When I was about five years old, I remember waking up in the middle of the night and trying to get out of bed to go to the bathroom. It was so dark and I felt to the right and there was wall, and to my head and there was wall and I turned around and felt to the left and wall again and the foot and there was wall. It seemed like there was a solid wall on every side of me. I reached out and I still remember the rough sand paint that scraped at me as I tried to escape. I started to cry because I felt like I was trapped. I was just turned around and confused in the dark but my Dad came and turned on the light so I could see that I was free the whole time. Believing you are surrounded makes for a strong prison. Jesus, the light of the world, has come to shine into your dark places and let you know you are already free. Just like the nation of Israel, God has made you an escape route for every place where you are trapped and surrounded.

The king of Syria wanted Elisha dead. **II Kings 6:14-17 (KJV)** *[14] Therefore sent he thither horses, and chariots, and a great host: and they came by night, and compassed the city about. [15] And when the servant of the man of God was risen early, and gone forth, behold, an host compassed the city both with horses and chariots. And his servant said unto him, Alas, my master! how shall we do?* It appeared they were surrounded and defeated. The enemy and fear and doubt and danger and depression were all around them. *[16] And he answered, Fear not: for they that be with us are more than they that be with them.* That servant saw Elisha and himself; he counted one, two. Are just the two of us more than the enemy? I don't think so. Those were hopeless odds, but that was only in the natural. Elisha did not need to see to believe but he knew his servant did not see in the spirit the way he did. *[17] And Elisha prayed, and said, LORD, I pray thee, open his eyes, that he may see. And the LORD opened the eyes of the young man; and he* *saw: and, behold, the mountain was full of horses and chariots of fire round about Elisha.* The truth was that they were surrounded by the Lord Himself and He rose up to defend them. You can never be outnumbered when you have God!

Matthew 1:23 (KJV) *[23] Behold, a virgin shall be with child, and shall bring forth a son, and they shall call his name Emmanuel, which being interpreted is, God with us.* The Complete Jewish Bible accentuates it by spelling it Immanu El. That means, with mankind, continually is the ever-present and the all-powerful God. Not God who was with us, but the perpetual now, the limitless God. When the danger is great the provision is greater. **Hebrews 13:5 (KJV)** *[5] ...for he hath said, I will never leave thee, nor forsake thee.* He promised, "I will never fail you or abandon you." When you feel like there is no hope, His hope surrounds you when it feels like there is only pain and sickness His healing surrounds you. When it feels like death has won Eternal life surrounds you. He who cannot lie said "I am with you always."

Mark 4:35-41 (KJV) *[35] And the same day, when the even was come, he saith unto them, Let us pass over unto the other side. [36] And when they had sent away the multitude, they took him even as he was in the ship. And there were also with him other little ships. [37] And there arose a great storm of wind,* *and the waves beat into the ship, so that it was now full. ³⁸ And he was in the hinder part of the ship, asleep on a pillow: and they awake him, and say unto him, Master, carest thou not that we perish? ³⁹ And he arose, and rebuked the wind, and said unto the sea, Peace, be still. And the wind ceased, and there was a great calm.* There was a great calm, to stop the great storm and the great fear that accompanied it. *⁴⁰ And he said unto them, Why are ye so fearful? how is it that ye have no faith? ⁴¹ And they feared exceedingly, and said one to another, What manner of man is this, that even the wind and the sea obey him?* Jesus did not see the storm, He saw the calm. He saw what was needed and provided by a loving Father. Do not look at the problem, recognize Emanuel is here. You are surrounded by God!

When faced with the choice of denouncing God or death, the three Hebrew children stood on their faith and refused to bow to pressure. They had no Jewish support group…they were strangers, captives in a foreign land. Everyone around them bowed to the idol, but they could not deny their God. They committed their all to a God they believed was faithful and He showed up. **Daniel 3:17-28 (KJV)** *¹⁷ If it be so, our God whom we serve is able to deliver us from the burning fiery furnace, and he will deliver us out of thine hand, O* king. *¹⁸ But if not, be it known unto thee, O king, that we will not serve thy gods, nor worship the golden image which thou hast set up. ¹⁹ Then was Nebuchadnezzar full of fury, and the form of his visage was changed against Shadrach, Meshach, and Abednego: therefore he spake, and commanded that they should heat the furnace one seven times more than it was wont to be heated. ²⁰ And he commanded the most mighty men that were in his army to bind Shadrach, Meshach, and Abednego, and to cast them into the burning fiery furnace. ²¹ Then these men were bound in their coats, their hosen, and their hats, and their other garments, and were cast into the midst of the burning fiery furnace. ²² Therefore because the king's commandment was urgent, and the furnace exceeding hot, the flame of the fire slew those men that took up Shadrach, Meshach, and Abednego. ²³ And these three men, Shadrach, Meshach, and Abednego, fell down bound into the midst of the burning fiery furnace. ²⁴ Then Nebuchadnezzar the king was astonied, and rose up in haste, and spake, and said unto his counsellors, Did not we cast three men bound into the midst of the fire? They answered and said unto the king, True, O king. ²⁵ He answered and said, Lo, I see four men loose, walking in the midst of the fire, and they have no hurt; and the form of the fourth is like the Son of God.* You will never know how much God loves you and how truly amazing He is until He is walking with you through the Fire. No matter what we face our God is enough...their God was enough. The fire had no power over them. *²⁶ Then Nebuchadnezzar came near to the mouth of the burning fiery furnace, and spake, and said, Shadrach, Meshach, and Abednego, ye servants of the most high God, come forth, and come hither. Then Shadrach, Meshach, and Abednego, came forth of the midst of the fire. ²⁷ And the princes, governors, and captains, and the king's counsellors, being gathered together, saw these men, upon whose bodies the fire had no power, nor was an hair of their head singed, neither were their coats changed, nor the smell of fire had passed on them. ²⁸ Then Nebuchadnezzar spake, and said, Blessed be the God of Shadrach, Meshach, and Abednego, who hath sent his angel, and delivered his servants that trusted in him, and have changed the king's word, and yielded their bodies, that they might not serve nor worship any god, except their own God.* They would not bend, they would not bow, they would not burn and God got the glory.

When told that praying to God meant death by means of a bunch of hungry lions, Daniel also trusted in God. Even more important than Daniel surviving a night surrounded by lions was the fact that the king and a heathen nation were watching and hoping that there really was a God who could deliver. **Daniel 6:19-23 (KJV)** *[19] Then the king arose very early in the morning, and went in haste unto the den of lions. [20] And when he came to the den, he cried with a lamentable voice unto Daniel: and the king spake and said to Daniel, O Daniel, servant of the living God, is thy God, whom thou servest continually, able to deliver thee from the lions? [21] Then said Daniel unto the king, O king, live forever. [22] My God hath sent his angel, and hath shut the lions' mouths, that they have not hurt me: forasmuch as before him innocency was found in me; and also before thee, O king, have I done no hurt. [23] Then was the king exceeding glad for him, and commanded that they should take Daniel up out of the den. So Daniel was taken up out of the den, and no manner of hurt was found upon him, because he believed in his God.* Daniel's faith and trust were met by the power of God and he was kept safe from harm. God proved that He could stop any force that opposed believers. If He did that in the Old Testament, under a lesser covenant, just think what He would do for us.

I remember hearing about a woman in a communist country, who had been arrested for being a Christian. She was thrown into a jail cell and her captors decided that they should teach her a lesson and have a little pleasure in the process.

Eight guards entered her cell, intent upon raping and beating her. They found her kneeling in prayer. They mocked her and taunted her, but she continued to pray. One of the men reached out and grabbed her shoulder. When he touched her, he pulled back his hand screaming in pain. The palm of his hand was blistered as if he had placed it on a hot stove. The men exited her cell and soon she was released unharmed. Yes, she had been surrounded, and yes they were strong and powerful and no one would have stopped them from abusing her. She could have crumbled in fear, but she knew that while she was indeed surrounded by the enemy she was also encircled in the arms of God. It was as if the fire of His presence formed a force field around her. No evil could touch her.

Isaiah 26:3-4 (KJV) *³ Thou wilt keep him in perfect peace, whose mind is stayed on thee: because he trusteth in thee. ⁴ Trust ye in the LORD for ever: for in the LORD JEHOVAH is everlasting strength:*

Peace and freedom are not based on circumstances. It is vitally important to see beyond our perception of the circumstances. The three Hebrew children were free while still in the fire; Paul was free while in prison. How you think affects you. David was already anointed as King of Israel while he fled from Saul. It is our right as believers to see danger and despair and then recon them smaller than the God who loves and encompasses us. **II Corinthians 10:5 (KJV)** *[5] Casting down imaginations, and every high thing that exalteth itself against the knowledge of God, and bringing into captivity every thought to the obedience of Christ;*

Isaiah 50:7-10 (KJV) *[7] For the Lord GOD will help me; therefore shall I not be confounded: therefore have I set my face like a flint, and I know that I shall not be ashamed. [8] He is near that justifieth me; who will contend with me? let us stand together: who is mine adversary? let him come near to me. [9] Behold, the Lord GOD will help me; who is he that shall condemn me? lo, they all shall wax old as a garment; the moth shall eat them up. [10] Who is among you that feareth the LORD, that obeyeth the voice of his servant, that walketh in darkness, and hath no light? let him trust in the name of the LORD, and stay upon his God.* That sounds a lot like Paul in his letter to the Corinthians.

II Corinthians 4:6-10 (KJV) *[6] For God, who commanded the light to shine out of darkness, hath shined in our hearts, to give the light of the knowledge of the glory of God in the face of Jesus Christ. [7] But we have this treasure in earthen vessels, that the excellency of the power may be of God, and not of us. [8] We are troubled on every side, yet not distressed; we are perplexed, but not in despair; [9] Persecuted, but not forsaken; cast down, but not destroyed; [10] Always bearing about in the* *body the dying of the Lord Jesus, that the life also of Jesus might be made manifest in our body.*

God more than meets our needs, just like He did with Hezekiah. In II Kings 20 Hezekiah was very ill then the prophet of God came in and said set your affairs in order you will die. Hezekiah did not look to the doctors; he did not look to his compassionate friends and family. The Bible tells us he turned his face to the wall and prayed. He turned away from all that death and sorrow and pain that encompassed him and looked only to God. In this circumstance all I see is God, and I have more than enough if I still see God as the answer. God is our help and His help really surrounds us. Hezekiah got to live fifteen more years; you can surely get your need met.

When they laid Jesus in the tomb, do you imagine the Father God in heaven fretting and fearful and seeing death as the end, NO! He knew what He had planned from the beginning. Jesus was defeating death once and for all. He was paying in full the sin debt of all men. When Jesus was dead and buried, God was setting the stage for the resurrection and Pentecost! He was setting the stage for your salvation and preparing for your victory too.

Psalm 121:1-8 (KJV) *¹ I will lift up mine eyes unto the hills, from whence cometh my help. ² My help cometh from the LORD, which made heaven and earth. ³ He will not suffer thy foot to be moved: he that keepeth thee will not slumber. ⁴ Behold, he that keepeth Israel shall neither slumber nor sleep. ⁵ The LORD is thy keeper: the LORD is thy shade upon thy right hand. ⁶ The sun shall not smite thee by day, nor the moon by night. ⁷ The LORD shall preserve thee from all evil: he shall preserve thy soul. ⁸ The LORD shall preserve thy going out and thy coming in from this time forth, and even for evermore.* It honors God when in the face of danger we look confidently to Him and know that His love surrounds us.

The Lord guards us. He protects us. Like a Seal team sent in to get us out of enemy territory, we are encompassed on every side, surrounded by a strong defense. The Lord is like those men who would take a bullet to protect the one they came to rescue; Jesus gets between us and the enemy. Being sensitive to, and aware of the One with you, helps you see past the obvious and the natural into the provision and the supernatural. The Lord has promised to turn our captivity and grant us peace when we place our full trust in Him. **Psalm 33:22 (KJV)** *²² Let thy mercy, O LORD, be upon us, according as we hope in thee.* The Living Bible puts it this way. **Psalm 33:22** *Yes Lord, let your constant love surround us, for our hopes are in you alone.*

Michael W. Smith has a song entitled *Surrounded.* The lyrics are "This is how I fight my battles, it may look like I'm surrounded, but I'm surrounded by you." I can hear Elisha singing that. I can hear Moses and Paul and Daniel singing it. I can hear the prisoner in the cell and the three Hebrew Children singing it. "It may look like I'm surrounded, but I'm surrounded by you."

In each of these cases, the odds were strongly against them. Without God's intervention, their chances of survival were zero. With God they were more than able to stand and win the victory. They may have stated with zero, but with God they were overcomers, victors, and examples for us to follow. Like Moses we can boldly say, *Fear ye not, stand still, and see the salvation of the LORD.* **[Exodus 14:13]**

Starting With Zero

Rev. Kathryn L. Smith

I Corinthians 13:9 (KJV) *⁹For we know in part…*

Starting With Zero

Lost Puzzle Pieces

On any given day, I might find a matchbox car or a giant Lego block or a few lost puzzle pieces under the table or between the cushions of my couch. Those are tell-tale markers that my great grandchildren were playing there. Those, along with countless tiny fingerprints and stale cheerios, leave me tired but also smiling. Those bits of evidence are not the whole story, but they are markers of where the story occurred.

In the same way, God shows us fragments of revelation so that we can catch sight of where He has been and what He has done. Some of those arbitrary puzzle pieces are clear parts of the picture of our lives. Others are so obscure we don't see how they fit in. **I Corinthians 13:9 (KJV)** [9] *For we know in part*...My experience tells me that even a puzzle piece that looks like nothing is important for completing the whole image.

I like to think about how God chose to fight idolatry in a dual between 450 prophets of Baal and one man of God. One with God verses 450 without; God likes those odds. Elijah took them on without fear. He challenged them to call down fire to consume their sacrifice, but nothing happened. Then he doused his bullock repeatedly with water so no one could say that it was possible to start a fire any way but through the supernatural power of God. He repaired the altar and prayed. **I Kings 18:36-39 (KJV)** *[38] Then the fire of the LORD fell, and consumed the burnt sacrifice, and the wood, and the stones, and the dust, and licked up the water that was in the trench. [39] And when all the people saw it, they fell on their faces: and they said, The LORD, he is the God; the LORD, he is the God.*

After years of drought and an outstanding victory against the forces of evil, Elijah promised rain. **I Kings 18:41-45 (KJV)** *[41] And Elijah said unto Ahab, Get thee up, eat and drink; for there is a sound of abundance of rain.* There was no cloud or thunder, Elijah heard it in the spirit. He had just called down fire from heaven, so there was reason to take his prediction seriously. *[42] So Ahab went up to eat and to drink. And Elijah went up to the top of Carmel; and he cast himself down upon the earth, and put his face between his knees,* He prayed earnestly to a God who could send both fire and rain. *[43] And said to his servant, Go up now, look toward the sea. And he went up, and looked, and* *said, There is nothing. And he said, Go again seven times.* ^{44} *And it came to pass at the seventh time, that he said, Behold, there ariseth a little cloud out of the sea, like a man's hand.* There is one tiny cloud that I can hide with my hand. It is just a tiny thing; it's nothing. *And he said, Go up, say unto Ahab, Prepare thy chariot, and get thee down, that the rain stop thee not.* ^{45} *And it came to pass in the meanwhile, that the heaven was black with clouds and wind, and there was a great rain.* Elijah was good at taking one tiny image cut out of the whole and seeing the big picture. That tiny cloud was a promise of a flash flood. He saw that one tiny cloud and recognized it would end the drought that had persisted for years. Sometimes we discredit what we see as too little to even amount to a promise of more.

Men of faith see more than the image in front of them; they see God at work. But even the most faithful believer gets tired and discouraged at times. Just a few days after his great victory, Elijah yielded to depression. That same prophet sat down and had a pity party complaining to God. "I have been faithful while they killed your prophets and now they want me dead too. I am the only one who has stood their ground." God corrected Elijah and told him how to move forward. God made sure that His prophet knew there would always be a remnant of faithful believers. [I Kings 19:18] He reminded Elijah to get his eyes off this tiny piece of the puzzle and look at the big picture.

Isaiah 40:28-31 (KJV) *[28] Hast thou not known? hast thou not heard, that the everlasting God, the LORD, the Creator of the ends of the earth, fainteth not, neither is weary? there is no searching of his understanding. [29] He giveth power to the faint; and to them that have no might he increaseth strength. [30] Even the youths shall faint and be weary, and the young men shall utterly fall: [31] But they that wait upon the LORD shall renew their strength; they shall mount up with wings as eagles; they shall run, and not be weary; and they shall walk, and not faint.* "When God is taking too much time to get you where you need to be, or when you think you have been backed against the Red Sea and face the hot breath of the enemy, be reassured that God has positioned you for a revelation of His power." (Fry p. 251) God knows your every need and He has made a way of escape or is giving you provision as you wait. Do not fear. Do not panic, God is preparing you to go from a zero to an overcomer.

We must never limit what God can do for us or through us. **Ephesians 3:20-21 (KJV)** *[20] Now unto him that is able to do exceeding abundantly above all that we ask or think, according to the* *power that worketh in us, ^{21} Unto him be glory in the church by Christ Jesus throughout all ages, world without end. Amen.* He is more than enough to make up for any lack on our part.

I can't remember where I heard this story, but it is worth repeating. A very bored little boy came into his dad's den and wanted to play. The father was busy trying to finish up some important paperwork. When his son persisted in trying to get his attention, the father decided to give him something to do. He took a magazine off the shelf, cut up a picture of a world map creating a puzzle and gave it to his son. "Now when you get the whole world back together come and talk to me and we will go get an ice cream. While you do that I will finish my work." The boy ran off with the pieces of his puzzle and his dad got back to work. In just a few minutes the boy returned all smiles with the map back together. His dad looked at him in astonishment. "How did you do it so fast?" His son grinned, "There was a picture of a man on the back, so when I got the man right the world was right."

The truth is that if we get our own lives right; it does help set the world straight. Maybe it is just a small blue puzzle piece that you have found. It could be water or sky or part of a blue house, but if we get the pieces back where they belong, it will add to the whole and make the big picture something beautiful.

God is not trying to just keep us busy, and He doesn't want to raise independent children. He wants us to lean on Him. "God has wonderfully designed me as fundamentally incomplete—designed to find my completeness as I rightly relate to God and to others. Dependence is not weakness, it is owning up to the reality of things. It is an absolute reliance on God based not on our need alone, but on God's design in demonstrating His glorious power." **Hebrews 4:16 (KJV)** *[16] Let us therefore come boldly unto the throne of grace, that we may obtain mercy, and find grace to help in time of need.* "God cannot show Himself powerful to those who feel adequate and whose confidence is in their own abilities." (Fry 252) He isn't trying to make us weak or needy. God wants us to realize we are one with Him who is all and has all. He wants us to trust Him and come to Him in every situation so that the world will see His grace and love poured out.

I Corinthians 13:12 (KJV) *[12] For now we see through a glass, darkly; but then face to face: now I know in part; but then shall I know even as also I am known.* It is alright that I don't have it all together, that I do not know and understand everything. My success in life is never according to my ability or strength or knowledge but I have the Spirit of God inside me and that is enough! I might be a zero in someone else's eyes but one man or woman walking in unity with the All-knowing, All-

Powerful, Ever-present God is a majority that no enemy can defeat.

We don't have all the answers. We have a handful of puzzle pieces and a glimpse at what might be. We also have a Heavenly Father who loves us and equips us as needed.

Ecclesiastes 11:4 (KJV) *⁴ He that observeth the wind shall not sow; and he that regardeth the clouds shall not reap.* Never let the fear of what might happen stop you. What do you have in your hand? If it is a seed, then sow it. If it is an opportunity, take it; and if it is faith use it. We add our tiny seed of faith to take us from Zeros to the place where we experience the miraculous.

Works Cited

Beacon Bible Commentary. (Kansas City, MO. Beacon Hill Press, 1969) vol. 6 p. 89, vol.7. p 45, 46, 47.

Copeland, Kenneth. *The Laws of Prospereity.* (Fort Worth, TX: Kenneth Copeland Publications, 1974) p. 21, 23, 26.

Cymbala, Jim. *Fresh Power.* (Grand Rapids, MI: Zondervan, 2001) p. 16, 17, 18, 19, 30, 32, 39, 41.

Fry, Steve. *I Am, the Unveiling of God.* (OR: Multnomah Publishers, 2000) p. 62, 63, 64, 65, 251, 252.

Gower, Ralph. *The New Manners and Customs of Bible Times.* (Chicago IL: Moody Press, 1987) p, 109.

Hagin, Kenneth. *El Shaddai.* (Tulsa OK: Faith Library Publications, 1993) p. 3, 6.

Murray, Andrew. *The Power of the Blood and the Cross.* (Fort Washington, PA: CLC Publications, 2017) p. 14, 18, 19, 88.

Prince, Joseph, *Daily Grace Inspirtations* (Joseph Prince Ministries 4/20/18, 9/3/18)

Smith, Malcolm. *Lost Secret of the New Covenant.* (Tulsa, OK: Harrison House, 2002) p. 31, 61, 69, 88, 99, 102, 217, 228.

Stone, Perry. *Mystery of the Priesthood and the Blood.* (Cleveland, TN: Voice of Evangelism Outreash Ministries, 2007) p. 52, 82, 88, 167.

Tenney, Tommy. *God's Eye View.* (Nashville, TN: Thomas Nelson Publishers, 2002) p. 4, 7, 24, 25, 27, 28, 33, 40,

Rev. Kathryn L. Smith

Author Page

I was saved in 1972, in a revival at Suburban Baptist Church in Granite City IL. I learned to love the Lord and His Word and began my walk there. In 1980, I was filled with the Holy Spirit at Full Gospel Evangelistic Center of Alton. It was there that I began to minister the Word in Power. God called me to "Build up the body of Christ," and I have been preaching and teaching all these years for that purpose. Becoming an author was a natural expansion of that call to minister. I love teaching and preaching and there is no greater joy than walking the path He places before me. I serve locally as an associate minister at The House of Victory in Cottage Hills IL, under Pastor Timothy Naylor. I am available for speaking engagements and would gladly come minister at your church or conference.

Starting with Zero is my sixth book. If you were blessed by it, I would recommend that you read some of my others. <u>There is Fire in the Blood</u>, my first book, explores the blood sacrifices throughout time as they point to the Blood of Jesus and bring us the Fire of His presence. It was the same fire that fell on the sacrificial altars of Abel, Elijah, and Moses that produced the blaze of Pentecost. As we honor the blood and recognize its power we make way for the glory of God; if we want to experience the Fire, we know where to find it; 'There is Fire in the Blood.'

My second book, <u>Meet Me on the Mountain</u>, focuses on intimate fellowship with God. The mountain of God is that place where faith and hunger produce His presence. The drive to climb is not just man striving for God; it is an answer to the call. God loved us first and He is calling to the heart of man to draw nearer and stay longer in His presence. This book has more personal experiences included to demonstrate how He meets with us and longs for passionate fellowship with His children. If you seek Him—you will find Him.

My third book, <u>I Hear the Rocks Falling</u> was inspired by the woman caught in adultery and thrown at the feet of Jesus. She expected the stones to crush her. Instead she heard the sound of the rocks falling to the ground as her accusers left. Like her, most of us have had moments of despair and shame and condemnation. Repeated offences deepen our sense of loss stacking one harsh, hardened, hurtful memory on top of another until we are bound within an internal prison. Jesus speaks to all of us to come out of those walls. We are to walk free from all condemnation and everything that has kept us tied to our past.

<u>Wilt Thou Be Made Whole</u> is an invitation to receive healing. On the cross, Jesus purchased salvation, and freedom from every consequence of Adam's fall. Healing belongs to us. It is not something we are trying to grasp; it was purchased for us by virtue of His broken body and shed blood. When we recognize that He bore our sickness like He bore our sin, we can access His healing power. Every word of testimony and scripture in this book was purposed to raise your faith so that you too can be free from sickness and disease. He is still asking, "Wilt Thou Be Made Whole?"

<u>I Am Who God Says I Am</u> is the fifth book that I have authored. This book helps us to see ourselves through our identity in Christ. We are loved and valued so much more than most of us know. I pray that you will learn to trust confidently in who God says you are.

Contact information:

Fire in the Blood Ministries

Rev. Kathryn L. Smith

Email: klssaved1972@yahoo.com

Fire in the Blood Ministries also has a Facebook Page

fbm/revkathy   or   m.me/revkathy

www.ingramcontent.com/pod-product-compliance
Lightning Source LLC
Chambersburg PA
CBHW052056110526
44591CB00013B/2229